ADVENT/CHRISTMAS

INTERPRETING THE LESSONS OF THE CHURCH YEAR

BERNARD BRANDON SCOTT

PROCLAMATION 5 SERIES C

FORTRESS PRESS   MINNEAPOLIS

PROCLAMATION 5
Interpreting the Lessons of the Church Year
Series C, Advent/Christmas

Scripture quotations, unless otherwise noted, are from the New Revised Standard Version Bible, copyright © 1989 by the Division of Christian Education of the National Council of Churches of Christ in the U.S.A. and used by permission.

Cover and interior design: Spangler Design Team

Library of Congress Cataloging-in-Publication Data
(Revised for volume C, 2)

Proclamation 5.

    Contents: ser. A. [1] Advent/Christmas / Mark Allan
Powell — [2] Epiphany / Pheme Perkins — [etc.] —
ser. C. [2] Epiphany / Gail R. O'Day.
    1. Bible—Homiletical use.   2. Bible—Liturgical
lessons, English.   I. Perkins, Pheme.
BS534.5.P765   1994   251   92-22973
ISBN 0-8006-4193-0 (ser. C, Advent/Christmas)
ISBN 0-8006-4194-9 (ser. C, Epiphany)
ISBN 0-8006-4195-7 (ser. C, Lent)
ISBN 0-8006-4196-5 (ser. C, Holy Week)

The paper used in this publication meets the minimum requirements of American National Standard for Information Sciences—Permanence of Paper for Printed Library Materials, ANSI Z329.48-1984. ∞™

Manufactured in the U.S.A.   AF 1-4193

98   97   96   95   94   1   2   3   4   5   6   7   8   9   10

CONTENTS

First Sunday in Advent

Lutheran	Roman Catholic	Episcopal	Revised Common
Jer. 33:14-16	Jer. 33:14-16	Zech. 14:4-9	Jer. 33:14-16
1 Thess. 3:9-13	1 Thess. 3:12—4:2	1 Thess. 3:9-13	1 Thess. 3:9-13
Luke 21:25-36 or Luke 19:28-40	Luke 21:25-28, 34-36	Luke 21:25-31	Luke 21:25-36

FIRST LESSON: JEREMIAH 33:14-16

At the beginning of Advent, the readings offer us the opportunity to consider the end, for ironically the Lord's coming is both the beginning and the end. As T. S. Eliot wrote, in the end is the beginning. The first lesson occurs in a section of Jeremiah often referred to as the Book of Consolation (chaps. 30–33). These chapters, part prose and part poetry, overflow with hope and promise, whereas devastation, grief, and despair dominate the rest of the book.

Chapter 33 is a collection of prose oracles connected loosely by the theme announced in verse 3: "Call to me and I will answer to you, and will tell you great and hidden things that you have not known." Each oracle has a similar opening based on the formula "Thus says the LORD." Three of the sayings, vv. 14-16, 17-18, and 19-22, deal respectively with David, Jerusalem, and the priesthood, showing God's unfailing faithfulness to the covenant with the people. The first reading for the First Sunday of Advent forms the first of these three oracles, but one must explore its connection to the others in order to avoid distorting its sense.

The beginning of chapter 32 sets a historical context for the oracles that follow in chapters 32 and 33. The army of Nebuchadrezzar, king of Babylon, is besieging Jerusalem and the king of Judah, Zedekiah, has imprisoned Jeremiah for prophesying Jerusalem's downfall and Zedekiah's capture. This situation would date the oracle in 588 B.C.E. At this low point in Judah's fate, the prophet looks out into the future to prophesy God's ultimate faithfulness to the covenant.

But this context is apparently fictional. The three oracles in verses 14-26 are the longest continuous section of Jeremiah absent from the Septuagint (LXX), the ancient Greek translation of the Hebrew Bible.

Thus it may have become part of the Hebrew textual tradition some time later than the historical context would indicate. There are other reasons for positing a later date. As William Holladay, in his magisterial commentary on Jeremiah, has noted, the Hebrew itself appears to be of a later type, indicating a postexilic date (*Jeremiah 2*, Hermeneia [Minneapolis: Fortress Press, 1989], 228).

The oracle in verses 14-16 parallels one in Jer. 23:5-6. A later scribe recycles an earlier oracle from Jeremiah by importing it into the post-exilic period. In recycling the earlier oracle, the new name given by God, "The LORD is our righteousness," undergoes a shift. In Jeremiah 23 this name given by the Lord involved a wordplay. The Hebrew terms translated "righteousness" and "Zedekiah" (King of Judah, 597– 587 B.C.E.) contain the same Hebrew root (*sedeq*). Zedekiah had received his name from the foreign king as a sign of his legitimacy (2 Kings 24:17). Now this new name indicates God's future legitimacy for the Davidic line. In Jeremiah 33, the city of Jerusalem takes the place of the king and the city receives the name. In the two oracles that follow this one, God confirms the covenant with David (33:17) and then with the Levites (33:18). Messianic hope is not vested exclusively in the Davidic line but also in the Levitical lines, the priesthood. This dual line reaffirms the covenant with Israel and Judah, the whole people. Thus the final oracle in this series (vv. 23-26) reaffirms that the Lord will never abandon God's people nor void God's covenant.

The use of this reading in the lectionary may appear to suggest that Jer. 33:14-15 is a messianic prophecy referring to Jesus, but that interpretation does not fit the biblical context. The REB reads unfor-tunately that the name will be given to "*him*," whereas the best reading of the Hebrew is "*her*," in reference to Jerusalem (NAB and NRSV translate "it," i.e., Jerusalem). Since this text is missing from the LXX, it could play no role in the development of Christian messianism in the Greek New Testament. Indeed, no clear reference to the text occurs in Christianity until the medieval period.

The reading makes a number of important points. The recycling points out the fluidity of God's word. The word of God is for God's people and is always in need of recycling. As to how one tests the validity of that recycling, the reading offers some important sugges-tions. God's word is one of hope. This oracle was recycled in a period of hopelessness, when the house of David was vacated and the temple empty. Yet the prophet remains convinced that God will honor the covenant. Israel and Judah will be saved. Christian messianism must remember this point, lest it rush to void the earlier covenant with Israel and usurp the promise for itself.

The prophetic promise paradoxically makes God present precisely in the moment when God is most missed, most absent. God's presence does not lie in some postponed future, but the future makes a claim on the present. God's covenant consists in "justice and righteousness," and, since it applies to both the Davidic and the Levitical lines, it involves what we would call the profane and the sacred. The promise of justice and righteousness, of a city in which to dwell by the name of "the LORD is our righteousness," stands in judgment on the present. The prophetic word makes God present in the experience of God's absence.

SECOND LESSON: 1 THESSALONIANS 3:9-13

The second lesson comes from what is probably the oldest writing in the New Testament, Paul's first letter to the Thessalonians. Written as early as the forties C.E., this is one of the few letters from Paul that does not combat some problem in the community. Rather, Paul appears to miss his new converts and writes to reassure them, to make contact with them, and incidentally to answer some questions about the day of the Lord that Timothy has relayed to him (5:1-11).

This early letter provides a glimpse of a newly born Christian community, with no tradition to fall back on except Paul's recent proclamation and catechesis. As the letter indicates, this community is focused on the Lord's future coming. Paul ends the thanksgiving with this summary of their Christian life: "how you turned to God from idols, to serve a living and true God, and to wait for his Son from heaven, whom he raised from the dead—Jesus, who rescues us from the wrath that is coming" (1:9-10). Paul's answers concerning the day of the Lord at the letter's end return to this theme. "May the God of peace himself sanctify you entirely; and may your spirit and soul and body be kept sound and blameless at the coming of our Lord Jesus Christ. The one who calls you is faithful, and he will do this" (5:23-24).

The second reading forms part of what has been termed Paul's apostolic parousia (coming). This formal element recurs in every Pauline letter. The apostolic parousia normally involves (1) the reasons for Paul's writing, then (2) the basis for his relation with the community, (3) the main part in which he details his efforts to be present to the community, (4) a prayer for God's approval of his efforts, and finally (5) the benefits that will accrue as a result of his apostolic presence. Since Paul intends to maintain contact with the community while in distress (3:7), the apostolic parousia takes on a central aspect. According to Robert Funk, Paul sees his presence to the community "under three different but related aspects at once: that of the letter, that of the apostolic emissary, and that of his own personal presence" (*Parables and Presence* [Philadelphia: Fortress Press, 1982], 82). The first two aspects, the letter and the emissary, substitute for his personal presence.

In terms of the apostolic parousia's formal outline, the second reading comes from parts 4 (prayer) and 5 (benefits). Verses 9 and 10 are Paul's prayer, while verses 11-13 detail the benefits of his presence.

The prayer begins as a thanksgiving, the normal form of Pauline prayer. We tend to view prayer as petition in which we ask God for something. But thanksgiving is so fundamental to Paul's understanding of prayer and thus the Christian stance toward life that it becomes itself a formal element in the Pauline letter. These formal thanksgivings are for the vitality of the community's faith, as in First Thessalonians. "We always give thanks to God for all of you and mention you in our prayers, constantly remembering before our God and Father your work of faith and labor of love and steadfastness of hope in our Lord Jesus Christ" (1:2-3). As part of the thanksgiving Paul includes the triad faith, love, and hope that demonstrates the integral connection between thanksgiving and Christian life. The formal thanksgiving also refers frequently to the parousia, as we have already seen in First Thessalonians. Nothing can stand in the way of thanksgiving for Paul, not even prophecy or speaking in tongues. As he asks in 1 Cor. 14:16-17, if one speaks in tongues how can "an outsider say the 'Amen' to your thanksgiving, since the outsider does not know what you are saying? For you may give thanks well enough, but the other person is not built up." Again Paul points out that the purpose of thanksgiving is love, building up the community.

In the apostolic parousia in First Thessalonians this same configuration develops around Paul's thanksgiving to God for all the joy he feels because of the Thessalonians. This joy draws out of him a prayer of thanksgiving, and he asks (petitions) that God "restore whatever is lacking in your faith" (3:10). Thanksgiving is the proper mode for prayer because it emerges from the understanding of God as Creator. We give thanks to God for creation.

Faith creates a mutual joy in the love of one another. Paul turns to this aspect in the next part of the apostolic parousia, which deals with the benefits of his presence. Those benefits are that "the Lord make you increase and abound in love for one another and for all, just as we abound in love for you" (3:12). The apostolic parousia functions to support not authoritarianism, but the sharing of love among the apostle and the community members.

The final benefit noted is Jesus' parousia (coming) "with all his saints" (3:13). This note completes the triad with the Thessalonians' hope to be found blameless at the parousia. For Paul this blamelessness is not an activity or an innate feature of the Thessalonians but a gift of God, who strengthens their hearts.

Paradoxically, both Paul and Jesus are absent; their coming (parousia) is in the future. Yet they are both present to the community—Paul by means of his emissary and his letter and the Lord Jesus in the community's very faith, hope, and love.

GOSPEL: LUKE 21:25-36

The first reading from Jeremiah 33 was recycled from an earlier oracle of Jeremiah, and the Gospel reading likewise is recycled from the apocalyptic discourse in the Gospel of Mark. As in the Jeremiah reading, the Gospel recycling produces some important shifts in the text. The most important difference between the Markan and Lukan versions of Jesus' last apocalyptic speech is that Luke severs the connection between the destruction of Jerusalem and the end of the world. Mark introduces the descriptions of the world's end by the phrase "in those days" (Mark 13:24), thus indicating that the last days of Jerusalem coincide with the world's end. Luke distances the recent events in Jerusalem from the world's end by the use of a simple future tense, "There will be . . ." (Luke 21:25), and also by shifting the speech's context. In Mark, Jesus addresses a small group of disciples, while looking across the valley at the Temple hill. His speech is a revelation, private and esoteric. In Luke, the speech takes place in the Temple as a public address; it is not secret knowledge that only the elect possess.

Today's Gospel, which concludes the apocalpytic sermon, has three parts: a description (vv. 25-28), a secular analogy (29-33), and a charge to watch out (34-36). These three units create a unified conclusion to the apocalyptic discourse.

The description of the world's end draws on the standard images from Jewish apocalyptic literature. Unconcerned about the time of the end—the *when*—Luke's Jesus accents its effect: "People will faint from terror at the prospect of what is coming over the civilized world, for the heavenly forces will be shaken!" (21:26, Scholars Version). This terror upon the whole civilized world (*oikoumenē*), unique to Luke's version of the sermon, plays to a major theme in the Gospel: that Christian faith has an effect in the political arena. For this reason to translate *oikoumenē* as "world," as the major translations do, misses its resonances in the Gospel of Luke. It means the inhabited world, the sphere of political activity, and frequently it signifies the Roman Empire. It is a more specific term than *kosmos*. Because Luke sees an intersection between the Empire's and the Christian stories, he employs the elaborate dating system at Jesus' birth to tie it to the events and rulers of his day. In the Magnificat Mary warns that the powerful will regret this birth.

When the Christian community sees the Son of man coming in power, they are to "stand up and raise [their] heads, because redemption is drawing near" (21:28). The Greek word translated "redemption" means deliverance or, as the REB has it, "liberation." The Christian community should not quake in fear and foreboding at the coming judgment, as the world does, but rejoice and stand tall.

The conclusion's second section uses an analogy (parable) drawn from nature to make the point about discerning the end time. We discern it in the same way that we discern the approach of summer. When the sap runs in the fig tree and it sprouts leaves, then we infer that summer is coming. So it is with the coming of the Son of man. He will come in due season; one should dispense with all esoteric speculation, of which Christians seem to be so fond these days.

As part of the analogy, Jesus issues a prophetic word that "this generation" will not pass away until all this has happened (v. 32). This saying has perplexed commentators for centuries. If "generation" refers to Jesus' contemporaries, then Luke, writing in the late eighties C.E., knows the saying did not come true. Why does he repeat it? Some commentators try to avoid this problem by arguing that "generation" refers to Luke's present readers, but this argument has weaknesses. First, it does not make literary sense. The readers of Luke's Gospel would naturally think that "generation" refers to those to whom Jesus is speaking, that is, his own contemporaries, just as modern readers do. Second, Luke indicates elsewhere that the coming of the kingdom remains in the distant future. For example, as Jesus and the disciples approach Jerusalem, he tells them the parable of the nobleman who goes into a far country and entrusts his estate to his servants. The narrator introduces the parable by remarking, "He went on to tell a parable, because he was near Jerusalem, and because they supposed that the kingdom of God was to appear immediately" (19:11). This is one of many signals in the Gospel that the kingdom is not near. Why then the confusing reference to "this generation"? Because Luke wants to undercut speculation on the end time. If one can make no obvious sense of the reference, then one should stop speculating until all is as clear as the budding of the fig tree. The coming of the kingdom is not esoteric but obvious.

The final section of the sermon's conclusion is unique to Luke's version of the apocalyptic discourse. Jesus warns the community to be on guard, not to be absorbed by dissipation or daily cares. One should not let the heart be weighed down, dulled, because the heart is the seat of life in ancient anthropology. The Christian stance is not to withdraw but to be on guard, to be alert, so that when the Son of man comes, one can stand up before him (cf. v. 28). The Christian does not fear the judgment or the coming of the Lord, but is on the alert, confidently expecting the end.

Second Sunday in Advent

[handwritten annotations in top right margin: "whole chapter hymn after glory...beauty...holiness... awe... Israel"]

Lutheran	Roman Catholic	Episcopal	Revised Common	
Mal. 3:1-4	Bar. 5:1-9	Bar. 5:1-9	*143* Bar. 5:1-9 or *995* Mal. 3:1-4	
Phil. 1:3-11	Phil. 1:4-6, 8-11	Phil. 1:1-11	*209* Phil. 1:3-11	
Luke 3:1-6	Luke 3:1-6	Luke 3:1-6	*61* Luke 3:1-6	

[handwritten marginal notes beside Revised Common column: "before purify", "TG, longing antithesis", "messiah", "John crying in the wilderness"]

FIRST LESSON: MALACHI 3:1-4; BARUCH 5:1-9

Malachi was active in the first half of the fifth century B.C.E. during the reign of Xerxes I. Although the temple had recently been restored under the control of the Zadokite priesthood, in the prophet's judgment the priesthood had degenerated. He accuses the priesthood of despising the Lord's name (1:6) and offering polluted sacrifices. The restoration of the Temple, which the prophets Haggai and Zechariah had strongly supported, has turned to bitter fruit in the prophecy of Malachi.

The first lesson belongs to a unit (2:17—3:5) that deals with the fundamental question of theodicy. The prophet turns his attention to a question that has plagued the great religious thinkers from Job onward. The people are complaining, "All who do evil are good in the sight of the LORD, and he delights in them" (2:17). How is it that the evil folks appear to prosper, when the good do not? Has God blessed the evil and cursed the good? "Where is the God of justice?" (2:17).

Malachi resorts to the solution of traditional apocalypticism. "See, I am sending my messenger to prepare the way before me, and the LORD whom you seek will suddenly come to his temple" (3:1). At the appropriate time the Lord will appear and set all things aright.

There has been considerable debate about the identity of the messenger who will prepare the way of the Lord. Some have argued that it is Elijah; at the book's conclusion, the Lord does promise to send "Elijah before the great and terrible day of the LORD comes" (4:5). This identification led early Christianity to identify the messenger with John the Baptist. But it is not clear that Malachi intended such an identification. He may have had in mind a priestly messenger, because in the next sentence he mentions "the messenger of the covenant" (3:1) and earlier in the book he describes the covenant of Levi as the ideal

11

priestly covenant (2:4-7). He surely looks forward to the restoration of this covenant. The expectation may be nonspecific, since messianic expectations in this period were fluid and unfocalized. Indeed, the prophet himself may be the forerunner; the word translated as "Malachi" (*mal'ākî*) means "my messenger"; hence one could translate: "The word of the LORD to Israel by my messenger." Throughout Israelite history messianic speculation varied, and Christian belief in Jesus' messiahship made the tradition appear in retrospect more solid and fixed than it was.

The day of the Lord will bring a purified priesthood and worship of Yahweh in the Temple. "Then the offering of Judah and Jerusalem will be pleasing to the LORD as in the days of old and as in former years" (3:4).

In the prophecy of Malachi, the messenger responds to the question of theodicy. That response should warn us that we cannot always judge by exterior circumstances. Some surely judged the situation differently than Malachi. The Temple was restored, the priests of Zadok were offering sacrifices, and the nation prospered. Was this not God's blessing? Yet the prophet sees it otherwise: "I am sending my messenger to prepare the way before me." At the end of this unit the prophet in the name of the Lord returns to the ancient Yahwistic standard of ethical behavior. He will bear witness "against those who oppress the hired workers in their wages, the widow and the orphan, against those who thrust aside the alien, and do not fear me" (3:5). This ancient standard concerns the defenseless, those who need Yahweh's special protection. One who fears the Lord will take care of them. That behavior will remain the standard of judgment on the day of the Lord.

The book of Baruch introduces itself by claiming to be the writing of Baruch son of Neriah during the fifth year of the exile of the Judeans in Babylon. The historical Baruch was the companion and scribe of Jeremiah. But one can adduce many reasons to question this identification and to see the book as an example of pseudepigraphy, one person writing in the name of another. According to Jer. 43:5-7, Baruch accompanied Jeremiah into exile in Egypt, not Babylon. No other evidence points to Baruch being in Babylon. Furthermore, the book has many historical inaccuracies and the situation reflects the later practices of Maccabean times (200–60 B.C.E.). For example, fasting and prayer commemorating the capture of the Jerusalem described in

Irony: the use of word to convey the opposite of their literal meaning / contrast between apparent and intended meaning / incongruity between expected & actual outcome

Bar. 1:5ff. remind one of Jewish customs in the Second Temple period. Also the book freely employs segments of other biblical books (especially Job, Daniel, and Isaiah) to construct its prophecies. The Maccabean period was a time of intense conflict in Israel and an unknown prophet remembers a past situation in which Jerusalem was lost and eventually restored, on which he bases a call for hope. This recycling and imaginative use of God's past dealings with the people as a basis for understanding the present is typical of the postexilic or scholastic period of Israelite prophecy.

Sometimes this book is referred to as First Baruch to distinguish it from *Second* and *Third Baruch*, which do not appear in the canon (see James H. Charlesworth, ed., *The Old Testament Pseudepigrapha, Vol. 1, Apocalyptic Literature and Testaments* [Garden City, N.Y.: Doubleday, 1983], 615–80, for translations of these noncanonical works). Many Christian churches do not recognize the canonical character of (First) Baruch because it is not contained in the Hebrew canon, although it was surely written originally in Hebrew. The debate about which books are canonical revolves around a small number of books, sometimes called apocryphal or deuterocanonical, that the LXX includes along with the books from the Hebrew Bible. Because Greek was the dominant language, the early church accepted the LXX as its list of books, and in 1546 the Council of Trent decreed Baruch among the canonical books. Under the influence of Renaissance scholarship, the Reformers returned to the Hebrew Bible as the "original" canon and thus excluded those books from the LXX tradition that were not part of the Hebrew Bible.

This first lesson comes from the book's conclusion, a long poem that is a pastiche of phrases from Isaiah 40–55. The beginning of the poem makes its purpose clear. "Take heart, my people, who keep Israel's name alive. You were sold to the heathen, but not to be destroyed" (4:5-6, REB). The whole poem encourages Israel in exile not to lose heart. The poem's conclusion uses Jerusalem in a metonomy for the people: Jerusalem takes off the garment of sorrow and affliction and is clothed with a robe of righteousness and a crown of glory (5:1-2). Neither of these actions is Jerusalem's doing but God's. God's righteousness and glory adorn the holy city. The city will receive a new name, "Righteous Peace, the Splendour of Godliness" (5:4 REB). With Jerusalem resplendently clothed in divine garments and given a divine name, God tells the city to see its exiled children returning. The long

pastiche: dramatic, literary, musical piece openly imitating the previous work of another artist, often with satirical intent irony, derision, wit to expose folly or wickedness

13

exile of misery is over. Drawing phrases from Isa. 42:16-17 Baruch states: "God has ordered that every high mountain and the everlasting hills be made low and the valleys filled up, to make level ground, so that Israel may walk safely in the glory of God" (Bar. 5:7).

This poem of a restored Jerusalem and Israel as well as the alternative first reading from Malachi remind us of the permanence of God's covenant with the people of Israel. In these days of Advent as we prepare for the Lord's coming, it is important for gentile Christians to reflect on God's covenant with Israel. Can it be superseded? Can it be set aside? In his Letter to the Romans Paul addresses this issue. He makes several moves that would allow him to evade the issue, but never does. For example, in the letter's first part he argues that true circumcision is not that of the flesh, but "a person is a Jew who is one inwardly, and real circumcision is a matter of the heart" (Rom. 2:29). Such an expansive definition of circumcision would allow him, one would think, to do away with the people of Israel and replace them with "real" Jews, the believing Gentiles. Yet he refuses this line of argument. "What if some were unfaithful? Will their faithlessness nullify the faithfulness of God? By no means! Although everyone is a liar, let God be proved true" (3:3-4). In Paul's logic God's essence is fidelity. Otherwise, God would not be God.

In contemplating the Messiah's birth, a Messiah for the people of Israel, we Gentiles need to ask ourselves about the value of the promises of the new covenant if those of the old covenant are voided. What guarantee have we that God will keep the new promises if God vacates the old promises? "So I ask, have they [Israel] stumbled so as to fall? By no means! But through their stumbling salvation has come to the Gentiles, so as to make Israel jealous" (11:11). We bear then an awesome responsibility. We are so to exhibit the promises and gifts of God as to make Israel jealous. If they are not, whose fault is it?

SECOND LESSON: PHILIPPIANS 1:1-11

Both first readings were written from a perspective of hope during a time of crisis, both looking forward to the day of the Lord's coming in which all will be restored. They both are the cry of hope of one near despair at the discrepancy between what ought to be and what is. The second reading comes from Paul's Letter to the Philippians, written while he was in prison. All three readings, despite their tone of hope, have as an undertow the price that following God may at times demand from us.

Philippi was a city in Macedonia that Roman colonists had resettled and constituted on the model of a Roman city. This strong Roman influence was reinforced by the city's prominent position on the Via Ignatia, the major Roman road connecting Asia and Italy. It was one of the first cities in which Paul, Timothy, and Silas made converts after crossing from Asia into Europe. Acts 16:11-40 records Paul's activity there. Lydia, a purple-dye merchant, was prominent in the Christian community of Philippi.

It is difficult to date the letter because several of Paul's imprisonments would fit the letter's details. It could have been written in the fifties, or perhaps as late as Paul's Roman imprisonment in the early sixties.

The second reading forms the letter's thanksgiving. A thanksgiving is part of all Paul's letters except Galatians. The thanksgiving appears to be a distinctive creation of Paul's letter-writing style that replaces the health wish found in many private letters of the time. The following example typifies the opening of a private, ancient letter. "Atremidoros to Zenon greeting. If you are well, it would be excellent; I myself am also well and Apollonios is healthy and everything else is satisfactory" (John L. White, *Light from Ancient Letters*, Foundations and Facets [Philadelphia: Fortress Press, 1986], 50). Thanksgiving is also a primary form of Jewish prayer and central in the Pauline understanding of prayer.

Despite Paul's imprisonment he prays with joy, an emotion that pervades most of this letter. As in Paul's other letters, the thanksgiving announces subtly the letter's major theme. In Rom. 1:5 Paul is thankful for the Philippians' sharing (NRSV), or partnership (NAB), or "the part you have taken" (REB). These translations are all trying to find an adequate English expression for the Greek *koinōnia*. "Association, communion, fellowship, close relationship" are among the glosses suggested by Walter Bauer (*A Greek-English Lexicon of the New Testament and Other Early Christian Literature*, trans. W. F. Arndt and F. W. Gingrich, 2d ed., rev. F. W. Gingrich and F. W. Danker [Chicago: Univ. of Chicago Press, 1979], 438). The word is frequently used of marriage as the most intimate relationship between human beings. So when Paul is thankful for the Philippians' *koinōnia*, he signals more than thanks for economic support. He is thanking God for the Philippians' intimate partnership/marriage in the gospel's proclamation.

Koinōnia

Furthermore, this partnership has existed from the first time they believed until now, and Paul is sure that this partnership will never be broken. The allusive phrase "the one who began a good work among you" (v. 6) is a Jewish way of avoiding the name of God. Thus this partnership was from the beginning, has been maintained until now, and will find its completion in the day of Christ Jesus' return.

Partnership becomes the overarching metaphor of this thanksgiving. This metaphor is appropriate for the Philippians. As a Roman colony they were undoubtedly familiar with the Roman custom of forming a *societas*. Paul Sampley defines a *societas* "as a legally binding, reciprocal partnership or association, freely entered upon between one person and one or more other persons regarding a particular goal or shared concern" (*Pauline Partnership in Christ: Christian Community and Commitment in Light of Roman Law* [Philadelphia: Fortress Press, 1980], 13). The Greek term for *societas* was *koinōnia*, hence Paul's use of the term here in the thanksgiving. The Philippians and Paul belong to a *societas* that binds them together in mutual support of the gospel's common goal. This theme of partnership also runs throughout the letter. At its conclusion, Paul thanks the Philippians for supporting him financially (4:10-20); and in the famous Philippians hymn (2:6-11) Paul tells them to have "among yourselves the same attitude that is also yours in Christ Jesus" (2:5, NAB). Thus Christ becomes the pattern of the Christian, the ultimate form of sharing.

Paul writes that "you hold me in your heart" (v. 7). In Greek this phrase is ambiguous, since one can also translate it "I hold you in my heart." One cannot determine what the Greek should mean here; given the theme of sharing/partnership in the thanksgiving, perhaps Paul intended the double meaning. The word *koinōnia* recurs in verse 7 with the suffix *syn* (with). The Philippians are copartners in his imprisonment and defense of the gospel. "Copartner" conveys the Greek's redundancy. The paraphrase translation of the REB catches the sense of the Greek: "Both while I am kept in prison and when I am called on to defend the truth of the gospel, you all share in this privilege of mine."

Other words of sharing/partnership occur in the thanksgiving. Paul longs for them, as Jesus longs for them (v. 8). Greek *splanchna* is variously translated: "compassion" (NRSV) seems less satisfactory than "deep yearning" (NEB) and "affection" (NAB). *Splanchna* is literally one's bowels and figuratively the seat of deep emotions. Hence Paul compares his longing for the Philippians to the deep emotional attachment of Christ to the Philippians. Thus he paints a picture of a deep emotional bond among apostle, community, and Jesus, all linked in a sharing/partnership, a *koinōnia*.

This image concludes when Paul states that he is praying "that their love may grow yet more and more" (v. 9, my translation). Love is the primary virtue for Paul that summarizes the believer's life. "Now faith, hope, and love abide, these three; and the greatest of these is love" (1 Cor. 13:13). Furthermore, this love enables the Philippians to decide what to do. Love produces knowledge and insight into the present situation and inclines toward action, not sentiment, as its description in 1 Corinthians 13 makes clear.

The purpose of this life of love is that "you may be pure and blameless, having produced the harvest of righteousness" on the day of the Lord (Phil. 1:10-11). Like most Pauline thanksgivings, this one concludes with a reference to the eschatological end. But the language is borrowed from the temple cult. "Pure," "blameless," and "harvest" (literally, "fruit") describe the perfect temple offering (see, for example, Malachi's depiction).

Paul began by giving God thanks and he concludes with a doxology: "for the glory and praise of God." This movement from thanksgiving to doxology describes the Pauline vision of life and creation. All of life gives thanks to God for life, and life is lived for the praise and glory of God. From thanksgiving to doxology is a movement of partnership that encompasses all of creation in God's *koinōnia*. "So if anyone is in Christ, there is a new creation: everything old has passed away; see, everything has become new! All this is from God, who reconciled us to himself through Christ, and has given us the ministry of reconciliation; that is, in Christ God was reconciling the world to himself" (2 Cor. 5:17-19). This is the vision of the Lord's coming that Advent presents to us. It is not the coming of an individual Lord, a personal savior, to commune with my piety. *Koinōnia* is always with others, with creation. It is the new creation of God's reconciled world.

GOSPEL: LUKE 3:1-6

Perhaps the difficulty of preaching about a date causes many to skip Luke's synchronistic date that opens the Gospel reading. But the date plays an important role in the Lukan narrative, by marking the beginning of the gospel story proper (see Acts 10:37), so that the previous stories of the birth form a prologue. For all the Synoptic Gospels, John the Baptist's preaching and baptizing signal the beginning of the gospel (Mark 1:1).

The date not only marks the story's beginning but also sets a tone and the stage. If its purpose was to provide a precise date, it has failed, because the intersecting reigns of the emperor, governors, and chief priests do not provide such a pinpoint. The "fifteenth year of the reign of Emperor Tiberius" is impossible to determine because we do not know which of the various available schemes Luke used to determine that point. (See Joseph Fitzmyer, *The Gospel According to Luke*, Anchor Bible 28A; 2 vols. [Garden City, N.Y.: Doubleday, 1981] 1:455–58, for details on issues of the time frame of the date.)

The mention of Tiberius, Pilate, Herod, and so on, and then Caiaphas and Annas denotes the secular and religious leadership that will have an impact on Jesus' and the believer's stories. This setting signals to the ancient reader that the events about to be narrated take place on a world stage, not on a local, private stage. The intersection between the new religion and the Roman Empire represents a primary theme of Luke's two-volume work. The consequences of the Messiah's coming go well beyond the private or regional sphere. They affect the world sphere, the *oikoumenē*, a prominent theme in last week's Gospel reading.

The date, with its secular formality, and the rolling phrases of its list, contrasts rhetorically with the simple introduction "the word of God came to John son of Zechariah in the wilderness" (3:2). Instead of the descriptive title "the baptist," Luke uses the patronymic title, which recalls the first episode in the prologue, the angel's message to Zechariah. The description of the word of God coming quotes the LXX of Jer. 1:1 (the LXX reverses the first two verses of the Hebrew text). Thus Luke sets John in the line of the great prophets. In his schema of salvation history John marks the end of the age of the law and the prophets and the beginning of a new age of the good news of the kingdom of God (Luke 16:16). As a prophet John's purpose is to announce God's word.

John is described as being in the "wilderness" (NRSV, REB) or "desert" (NAB). The symbolism of wilderness or desert in our culture differs from that of the ancient world. For us wilderness is a place of escape from the pressures of modern urban life. The wilderness symbolizes the frontier, the mythical space where America was born. The wilderness is a place where we might encounter a pure experience of

God. In the ancient world the wilderness meant uninhabited and there-fore dangerous space. It was a place of testing. The archetype of such symbolism was Israel's experience in the desert of Sinai during the years of exodus; there Yahweh tested the people before leading them into the promised land.

Luke quotes extensively from Isa. 40:3-5. Just as Baruch recycled a quotation, so here Luke recycles a quotation for a new prophetic usage. John is the voice crying out in the wilderness. Luke parallels the preaching of a baptism of repentance for the forgiveness of sins with the quotation from Isaiah. Luke 3:3-6 describe John's message and activity.

"Prepare the way of the Lord." The reference to "the Lord" is am-biguous. Does it mean God or Jesus? This same ambiguity is present in Zechariah's prophecy: "And you, child, will be called the prophet of the Most High; for you will go before the Lord to prepare his ways" (1:76). This ambiguity is probably deliberate, serving to fuse the presence of God with the presence of Jesus.

Luke extends the Isaiah quotation beyond Isa. 40:3, which the other Gospels quote, because of its last line: "and all flesh shall see the salvation of God." The line just quoted from the Benedictus is followed by a line with this same theme: "to give knowledge of salvation to his people by the forgiveness of their sins" (1:77). In both Zechariah's hymn and the introduction of John, Luke parallels salvation and the for-giveness of sins. Salvation is the coming of the kingdom. In Jesus' first speech in this Gospel, before his own people at the synagogue in Nazareth, he quotes from Isaiah: "The Spirit of the Lord is upon me, because he has anointed me to bring good news to the poor. He has sent me to proclaim release to the captives and recovery of sight to the blind, to let the oppressed go free, to proclaim the year of the Lord's favor." After finishing this reading Jesus announced, "Today this scrip-ture has been fulfilled in your hearing" (Luke 4:18-21). This is the forgiveness of sins, the voice crying in the wilderness, salvation, the coming of God's kingdom.

Third Sunday in Advent

Lutheran	Roman Catholic	Episcopal	Revised Common
Zeph. 3:14-18a	Zeph. 3:14-18a	Zeph. 3:14-20	Zeph. 3:14-20
Phil. 4:4-7 (8-9)	Phil. 4:4-7	Phil. 4:4-7 (8-9)	Phil. 4:4-7
Luke 3:7-18	Luke 3:10-18	Luke 3:7-18	Luke 3:7-18

FIRST LESSON: ZEPHANIAH 3:14-20

In the ancient church the Third Sunday of Advent was known as *Gaudete* Sunday (Rejoicing Sunday), after the first word in the Introit (the entering versicle), which was from Phil. 4:4, today's second reading. The readings for this day continue that ancient theme of joy at the nearness of the Lord's coming.

Zephaniah was a cultic prophet and probably a member of the group of prophets and Levites involved in the Deuteronomistic reform under King Josiah of Judah (640–609 B.C.E.). Our vision of what constitutes a prophet is dominated by the great prophets Isaiah and Jeremiah. The former was not a cultic prophet, while the latter broke with the cultic prophets. Combined with the tendency of the reformers to rail against the cult of the Roman Catholic Church, this vision of the prophets has left at times a prejudice against cultic prophets. Zephaniah is a vivid reminder of the power and vitality of Israel's cultic life and its reformative possibilities.

As a supporter of the Deuteronomistic reform under Josiah, Zephaniah calls for God's wrath against those who have fallen into idolatry and "dress in foreign apparel" (1:8, NAB). To those who have violated the covenant, he prophesies in the name of the Lord, "I will completely sweep away all things from the face of the earth" (1:2, NAB).

This first lesson comes from the book's conclusion, which pictures the new people of God, "a remnant in your midst, a people humble and lowly, who shall take refuge in the name of the LORD" (3:12, NAB). Some scholars have considered this concluding hymn a cultic hymn of celebration. The new Israel rejoices because the "LORD has taken away the judgments against you, he has turned away your enemies" (3:15). The prophet equates the Lord's judgment to victory by one's enemies, since such victory was frequently identified as punishment by God for the people's sins. God is addressed as king of Israel and a mighty warrior (NAB—"savior") who sings and dances with them as at a carnival. This beautiful anthropomorphic image of God cavorting with the remnant of Israel stands in sharp contrast to the avenging God of the book's first chapters. While the purpose of the attacking, destructive God is to produce the people's repentance, the dancing God truly excites and animates the prophet. With such a God one can truly "Sing aloud . . . shout. . . . Rejoice and exult with all your heart!" (3:14).

Some lectionaries continue the reading through verse 20. Most scholars consider this material to be later than Zephaniah's prophecies, probably added during the exile to update the prophecy after the failure of the Deuteronomistic reform and the carrying off of Judah into exile. Those in exile do not give up on the image of the playful, singing God, rejoicing with his people at carnival, but now add: "I will save the lame and gather the outcast, and I will change their shame into praise" (19). In exile the remnant learns to sympathize with the oppressed and outcast. But the eschatological hope remains: "At that time I will bring you home" (20). In the face of idolatry, oppression, and exile, the remnant people never lost faith in the image of the dancing and singing God.

SECOND LESSON: PHILIPPIANS 4:4-7 (8-9)

Philippians 4:4 was the versicle for the Introit of the Third Sunday in Advent in the ancient Roman liturgy, and its first word in Latin, *Gaudete,* gave the title to this Sunday. The second lesson comes from the letter's conclusion in a section that is generally referred to as parenesis (exhortation). This is a standard part of Paul's conclusion to a letter. Some sections of a parenesis are quite specific (see, for example, 4:2-3), while others are more general. Normally, both types of parenesis are mixed in the letters.

This general exhortation extends from verse 4 through verse 9 and exhibits a strong rhetorical and rhythmic style. The usually exemplary REB is unfortunately a particularly limpid translation. The NAB is probably the best. Here I offer my own translation to indicate the rhetorical structure.

Rejoice in the Lord always
I shall say it again: rejoice!
Your kindness should be *known* to all.

The Lord is near.
Have no anxiety at all,
but in everything
by prayer and petition and with thanksgiving
make your requests *known* to God.

Then the peace of God
that surpasses all understanding
will guard your hearts and [your] minds in Christ Jesus.

In the first strophe the second line reverses the first line (chiasm). In the second strophe the first three lines are very short and tight and the third has three balancing elements. The final lines of each strophe refer to "knowing" or "mind," tying together the three strophes. This strong rhetorical style continues in verses 8 and 9 with the repetition of "whatever is. . . ."

This lesson continues the rejoicing image of God found in the first reading. The approach of the Lord should produce not anxiety and worry but confidence and rejoicing. Why should the nearness of God be a moment of rejoicing? For the same reason that Zephaniah was confident. The true remnant need not fear the wrath of God because that wrath will be the peace of God that surpasses all understanding. For the remnant, wrath is living apart from God in idolatry.

GOSPEL: LUKE 3:7-18

If the first two lessons stress the joy in the Lord's coming, the third exposes a two-edged sword. The Gospel reading is divided into a three-part structure similar to that in Zephaniah: first, the preaching of the wrath of God against the people's offenses; second, advice as to what to do; finally, the promise of blessing at the Messiah's coming.

In Luke John addresses the crowds, not the Pharisees and Sadducees as in Matthew (Luke 3:7). We must be careful how we present this preaching today, because one can understand and proclaim it as anti-Semitic. In the background of John's preaching stand the Hebrew prophets. When John asks "Who warned you to flee from the wrath to come?" (3:7), the answer is "the prophets." "The wrath to come" is a reference to the day of the Lord. The symbol of the day of the Lord originated in the early tribal confederation of Israel, which celebrated God as a warrior who fought for Israel against its enemies. On the day of the Lord, God would destroy all Israel's enemies and exalt Israel above all its enemies (Obadiah 15). But the prophets turned this symbol around and used it against the wicked in Israel. "Alas for you who desire the day of the LORD! Why do you want the day of the LORD? It is darkness, not light; as if someone fled from a lion, and was met by a bear; or went into the house and rested a hand against the wall, and was bitten by a snake" (Amos 5:18-19).

John begins by calling the crowd (literally) "children of a snake" (Luke 3:7). This is clearly a slur that contrasts with their claim to have Abraham as a father. The "snake" may be a reference to the snake in the Garden of Eden. John rejects the claim that being a child of Abraham is sufficient to escape from the wrath on the day of the Lord. In this rejection he stands in the line of Israel's great prophets. The function of this preaching is not to prophesy Israel's rejection. The warning that the axe is lying at the root of the trees, even now, is just that—a warning. The purpose of this eschatological speech is to warn the people to repent (v. 8). Only those who do not bear fruit will be destroyed, not the whole people. We gentile hearers must pay attention to the speech's prophetic function; otherwise we may be tempted to hear this speech as a prophecy of Israel's rejection. John rejects salvation on the basis of a parental claim, a claim of inheritance, regardless of whom we have as a father—Abraham, Peter, Luther, George Washington, or even God. The criterion of salvation is that the tree must bear fruit.

In the second section John answers three questions to illustrate trees bearing fruit. The first answer involves sharing with those who have less. One who has two tunics in John's culture would be a person of wealth. A peasant would have only the clothes on her or his back. This advice parallels Jesus' advice to surrender your shirt if someone asks for your coat (6:29). In the second answer he tells toll collectors not to defraud anyone, a principle reflected also in the story of Zacchaeus (19:1-10). The position of both Jesus and John contrasts with that of the Pharisees, who considered collecting taxes an immoral, forbidden occupation and who would have demanded a renunciation of the trade. In the parable of the Pharisee and the Publican, the Pharisee rejects the publican because he is a publican. The Pharisees were strict in their ethics; John and Jesus were lax. The third situation deals with soldiers, probably mercenaries. Since Israel was an occupied territory, the Jews viewed soldiers negatively. Again, John's advice to soldiers is moderate: Don't extort money; be satisfied with your wages. In other words, do not run riot over a conquered territory.

The final section deals with messianism and the difference between John and Jesus. While John does not explicitly deny that he is the Messiah as in John 1:20, he implies that he is not.

We Christians are so used to applying the title Messiah or Christ to Jesus that we do not stop to ask ourselves what it meant. What did early Christians intend to affirm when they called Jesus the Messiah? The Hebrew word translated as "messiah" means "anointed," with the implication "by God." It was applied to priests and kings and came to mean by extension those appointed by God for a special mission. Thus Isa. 45:1 refers to Cyrus as "anointed" (messiah). For Isaiah to call Cyrus "messiah" is like George Bush calling Saddam Hussein Messiah instead of Hitler.

After the loss of the Davidic line, God's promise that David's house would be forever (2 Sam. 7:13-17; 23:5) led to the expectation of a new David to rule over Israel (Jer. 30:9). But none of the prophetic books speaks of a future messiah. The book of Daniel (9:25) mentions an anointed prince in association with the restoration of Jerusalem, but shows no other interest in this messiah prince.

The *Psalms of Solomon*, a first-century B.C.E. document, reflects the expectation of a future Davidic king who is described as God's Messiah. This ideal king reflects badly on the contemporary Hasmonean kings, who were non-Davidic. A few brief quotations from *Psalms of Solomon* 17 will give the narrative understanding of this Messiah.

> (4-5) Lord, you chose David to be king over Israel, and swore to him about his descendents forever, that his kingdom should not fail before you. But (because of) our sins, sinners rose up against us. . . . (21) See, Lord, and raise up for them their king, the son of David, to rule over your servant Israel in the time known to you, O God. . . . (30) And he will purge Jerusalem. . . . (32) And he will be a righteous king over them, taught by God. There will be no unrighteousness among them in his days, for all shall be holy, and their king shall be the Lord Messiah." (R. B. Wright, in James H. Charlesworth, ed., *The Old Testament Pseudepigrapha, Vol. 2, Expansions of the "Old Testament" and Legends, Wisdom and Philosophical Literature, Prayers, Psalms, and Odes, Fragments of Lost Judeo-Hellenistic Works* [Garden City, N.Y.: Doubleday, 1985], 665–67.)

From about the same period the Dead Sea Scrolls reflect a different view of the Messiah. The people of the scrolls were intensely involved in speculation about the end time, and they expected two Messiahs. Instructions concerning the community life inform the initiate: "They shall depart from none of the counsels of the Law to walk in the stubbornness of their hearts, but shall be ruled by the primitive precepts in which the men of the Community were first instructed until there shall come the Prophet and the Messiahs of Aaron and Israel" (1QS 9.9-11; Geza Vermes, *The Dead Sea Scrolls in English*, 3d ed. [London: Penguin, 1987], 74). These quotations from the *Psalms of Solomon* and the Dead Sea Scrolls indicate that in Jesus' time *messiah* was not a fixed, technical term—it was fluid. Similarly, expectations about the end time varied within Judaism. The expectation of a Messiah did not dominate Jewish life, nor did every Jewish mother pray to be the mother of the Messiah, contrary to what Christian piety has repeatedly asserted.

Furthermore, "Messiah" proved to be a problematic title for Jesus. The association with Davidic kingship and therefore political claims turned out to misinterpret Jesus. The Gospels never picture Jesus using the title as a self-designation; even in the case of Peter's confession, Jesus significantly reinterprets the title in the light of the suffering Son of man (Mark 8). Bruce Vawter's remark is to the point: "Christ is the primary faith-formula devised by early Christianity to designate its Lord and Savior, a formula it chose because none other would do and yet was so inadequate to the purpose that it had to be filled with new content" (*This Man Jesus: An Essay Toward a New Testament Christology* [Garden City, N.Y.: Doubleday, 1973], 97). Just as John rejected the title, so also Jesus avoided the title. As we look forward to the expectation of the Messiah's birth, we should reflect on the inadequacy of that title to describe God's activity in the Anointed rather than allow it to become a slogan we idolize.

John distinguishes himself from Jesus on the basis of their differing baptisms. John's baptism is one of water, a baptism of repentance for the forgiveness of sins that symbolizes the washing clean of the person. Jesus' baptism is one of "the Holy Spirit and fire." The Holy Spirit is God's breath (spirit), which gives life, and "fire" refers to the refining or purifying character of fire. Thus the baptism of Jesus differs from that of John in that it is a more powerful purification of the community.

Fourth Sunday in Advent

Lutheran	Roman Catholic	Episcopal	Revised Common
Mic. 5:2-4	Mic. 5:1-4a	Mic. 5:2-4	Mic. 5:2-5a
Heb. 10:5-10	Heb. 10:5-10	Heb. 10:5-10	Heb. 10:5-10
Luke 1:39-45 (46-55)	Luke 1:39-45	Luke 1:39-49 (50-56)	Luke 1:39-45 (46-55)

FIRST LESSON: MICAH 5:1-4

The prophet Micah was active in the last decade of the eighth century and was a contemporary of Isaiah. Some of his oracles appear to refer to Sennacherib's attack on Jerusalem in 701 B.C.E., when Jerusalem miraculously escaped capture. Many scholars also believe that his prophecies were reworked during the exile after Jerusalem fell in 587 B.C.E. Today's first reading probably reflects this mixed setting and is typical of the recycling that we have seen among the Hebrew prophets.

The prophecy concerning a ruler from Bethlehem is part of a group of three prophecies that all begin with "now." "Now why do you cry aloud?" (4:9). "Now many nations are assembled against you" (4:11). "Now you are walled around with a wall" (5:1 [4:14 NAB]). These oracles begin with a prophecy of devastation and end with a promise of hope and salvation. This pattern is frequent and normative in prophetic speech. Yahweh's devastation and punishment of Israel is never permanent, because God's character is marked by grace and love. As Jonah remarks when he attempts to avoid preaching doom on Nineveh: "That is why I fled to Tarshish at the beginning; for I knew that you are a gracious God and merciful, slow to anger, and abounding in steadfast love, and ready to relent from punishing" (Jonah 4:2).

The introduction to this third prophecy may refer either to the siege of Sennacherib or to the later Babylonian leveling of Jerusalem in 587 B.C.E. Perhaps an editor reworked the original prophecy of Micah to fit the postexilic period. In this prophecy Jerusalem and its present ruler represent the failed, sinful past, and Bethlehem and the new ruler represent the promised future. Bethlehem is held up as "one of the little clans of Judah" (Mic. 5:2) or "too small to be among the clans

26

of Judah" (5:1, NAB). This rags-to-riches theme is prominent in Hebrew storytelling. Moses protests: "Who am I that I should go to Pharaoh, and bring the Israelites out of Egypt?" (Exod. 3:11). The David and Goliath story again exemplifies this theme, with the added twist of small size versus great strength. David defeats Goliath, and the small and wily nation of Israel defeats the strong and wealthy Philistines.

The language of the prophecy is veiled and indefinite, giving it a mysterious air. Bethlehem is significant as the birthplace of David, although the passage does not mention a king but only a "ruler," a less definite term. The reference to the future ruler "whose origins are far back in the past, in ancient times" (5:2, REB) gives a mythical cast to the passage, and some have suggested it may refer to David *redivivus* (returned), similar to the expectation of Elijah's return. The rest of Israel returning (v. 3) appears to be a reference to the exile. But in the end the ruler shall "feed his flock in the strength of the LORD" (4a). The pastoral image again refers clearly to David, the shepherd who became Israel's king.

In this prophecy the Jews struggle to remain faithful to the covenant that God has given them. The covenant is a rags-to-riches story. Regardless of how hopeless things look, whether it is Sennacherib or Cyrus attacking Jerusalem, whether the people have been carried off into exile, whether the people have fully repented and turned to God, the prophet relies on God's faithfulness to the covenant made with Israel. From one of the little clans shall come a ruler to feed the flock of Israel.

SECOND LESSON: HEBREWS 10:5-10

The second lesson is of a very different type than the first. The Epistle to the Hebrews is a demanding exposition, probably the most demanding in the New Testament. Its Greek is among the best, indicating that its author has a superior education in the rhetorical schools. Its argument is not easy for us to follow, for it employs methods of exegesis that are foreign to us. Yet its intellectual contribution to Christianity is considerable because it explains and justifies the early Christian withdrawal from the Jewish sacrificial cult. Such a withdrawal was not an obvious move for Christians to make. According to Acts the early Christians participated in Temple activities, and when Paul returned to Jerusalem, he went first to the Temple to make his offering.

Yet when the Temple was destroyed, the early Christians did not long for its rebuilding. The Epistle to the Hebrews helps explain why.

The selection in today's reading is part of the conclusion (10:1-10) to the central argument in the letter. The author has drawn a strong distinction between the heavenly realm and the earthly realm and even explained the heavenly sacrifice of the new covenant. In this argument, the law is "a shadow of the good things to come, not the true picture" (10:1), as the REB idiomatically translates it. The very repetition of sacrifices indicates that they cannot be a perfect sacrifice. "But in these sacrifices there is a reminder of sin year after year. For it is impossible for the blood of bulls and goats to take away sins" (10:3-4). Thus the purpose of the blood sacrifice is to remind us of our sins.

The second lesson draws the conclusion of this inability of the law through its sacrifices to take away sins. Christ is the heavenly fulfillment of this earthly foreshadowing. The author imagines the words from Psalm 40 on the lips of Christ as he comes into the world. This speech is situated at the birth, not the death, of Jesus "because it indicates that the cosmos is the sphere of the decisive sacrifice of Christ" (Harold W. Attridge, *The Epistle to the Hebrews*, Hermeneia [Philadelphia: Fortress Press, 1989], 273). This context is especially significant given the negative view of the cosmos in comparison with the heavenly realm that has prevailed in the letter to this point (9:1).

Verses 5b-7 are a quotation with minor adjustments from the LXX of Psalm 40:7-9, which varies at some significant points from the Hebrew text. Verse 6b of the Hebrew text reads literally, "But ears you have dug for me," probably an idiom for obedience. The LXX translates this section of verse 6 as "you fashioned a body for me." In the exegesis of the psalm "body" plays a significant role for the author of Hebrews. The body of Christ prepared by God becomes the perfect sacrifice and offering in contrast to the sacrifices of the old order. According to the psalm quotation, God takes no pleasure in burnt offerings. It is important for us gentile readers of the text to understand that the argument here is not innovative but is drawn from the Hebrew Bible, the Torah, itself. The psalm is part of a well-established prophetic critique of cult. The body of Christ is the perfect offering because it is freely given, not coerced: "See, God, I have come to do your will" (Heb. 10:7). This offering too was foretold in the Torah, "the scroll of the book." I think the NRSV obscures the meaning of the text by putting the reference to the scroll in parentheses. This treatment makes it appear as an addition or afterthought, but it is a quotation from the psalm noting that both God's displeasure with burnt offerings and Jesus' freedom in doing God's will were foretold.

In the author's exegesis of the psalm, he uses technical legal language for what has happened. "He *abolishes* the first [burnt offerings] in order to *establish* the second" (v. 9). What is established is our sanctification "through the offering of the body of Jesus Christ once for all" (v. 10). What God wills is our sanctification, which is achieved by free obedience to the will of God as exemplified once for all in Christ's body. Because this obedience takes place in Christ's body, the heavenly sacrifice is united with the earthly sacrifice, thus overcoming the gulf between the two. Thus Christ's offering is unique and final. It cannot and does not need to be repeated, because the gap between heaven and earth has been closed. The perfect counter to sin is now clearly available to all.

The readings of Advent have frequently focused our attention on Jesus' final coming. Hebrews reminds us that the true end is the center—the death of Jesus. Jesus' death determines the end. Because of that death we will be able to stand up and not cower in fear at the Lord's coming. Likewise with the approach of Christmas, the Hebrews reading reminds us that when Jesus came into the world, it was with the offering of his body in mind.

GOSPEL: LUKE 1:39-49

The birth narratives of Jesus in general revolve around the activity of women. Zechariah does play a major role, but as an example of faith he provides a negative model. Mary provides the positive one, first in the angel's announcement of Jesus' conception, then in Mary's greeting of Elizabeth. Elizabeth is the first one besides Mary to recognize the significance of her pregnancy. This fiction of a familial relation between John and Jesus creates problems for other stories in the tradition. For example, if John and Jesus are cousins, why does John not know him at the baptism? Why does John send his disciples to inquire if Jesus is the one to come? They also seem to belong to different houses, John to a priestly house and Jesus to a Davidic one, at least according to tradition.

This story about Mary and Elizabeth illustrates the response of faith. The child leaping in the womb is a prophetic act demanding interpretation. When Rebekah is pregnant with Esau and Jacob, "the children struggled together within her; and she said, 'If it is to be this way, why do I live?' " (Gen. 25:22). The Lord tells her that this struggle in her womb means that the two nations born of these children will struggle. "The elder shall serve the younger" (Gen 25:23). Likewise when John jumps, Elizabeth, filled with the Holy Spirit, explains that it was "for joy," thus signaling what will be the relation between John and Jesus. It is not a struggle like that between Esau and Jacob; rather, John is the elder who will go before Jesus with joy.

Elizabeth's speech begins and ends with a beatitude for Mary. In the first Mary is blessed because of the fruit of her womb and in the second because she believes what the Lord has spoken to her. In both cases she is blessed for what is essentially the same thing: her faithfulness to God's word. The text makes no mention of Jesus as the Messiah here. The title is "Lord" *(kyrios)*, which is also used of God, as verse 45 makes clear. The LXX employs it to translate the tetragrammaton, the Hebrew name of God that was unspoken. *YHWH* represents in English alphabetic characters the Hebrew characters for the divine name. Devout Jews pronounce these consonants by means of the vowels of another divine name, *Adonai*, which also means "the Lord." *Jehovah* is a combination of the Hebrew consonants *(JHVH)* and the vowels of *Adonai*.

Recent scholarship on the Magnificat and the other hymns in the Lukan birth narrative has argued that they "are not so much pious prayers as they are revolutionary songs of salvation" (Richard A. Horsley, *The Liberation of Christmas: The Infancy Narratives in Social Context* [New York: Crossroad, 1989], 107). The three psalms or hymns in Luke's nativity narrative—the Benedictus, Magnificat, and Nunc Dimitis—find strong parallels in the Second Temple psalms such as those in Sirach, the Dead Sea Scrolls, or Judith 16. The late Second Temple period was a creative one in the development of Jewish psalmody. These three psalms undoubtedly had a prehistory in early Christianity prior to Luke incorporating them into their current narrative context. In the case of the Magnificat, one easily sees the narrative connection in verse 48. The beatitude responds to Elizabeth's greeting, and the reference to "the lowliness of his servant" echoes Mary's response to the angel. It also picks up on the rags-to-riches theme implied in the rest of the hymn and popular in Hebrew storytelling.

In Greek the psalm has a clear outline, divided into two strophes, verses 46-50 and 51-55. The lines are introduced by verbs (a structure that is not apparent in English translation): "magnifies" (46), "has done" (49), "has shown" (51; same Greek word as in 49), "brought down" (51), "has helped" (54). The subject of each of these verbs is the Lord, except for the initial one. Starting each line with a verb accents God's action. The parallel in the first strophe differs from that of the second. In the first strophe (vv. 46-50) the parallelism is synonymous—the same thing is repeated in different words.

> Because [he] has done for me great things the Mighty One,
>> and holy is his name,
> and his mercy is from generation to generation
>> to those who fear him.

This literal translation of verse 49 indicates the initial verb of action and the synonymous parallelism. The second strophe employs contrasting parallelism.

> He has brought down the mighty from their thrones,
>> and he has lifted up the lowly.

This combination of strong initial verbs and contrasts in the second strophe impart a sense of conflict and a world turned upside down.

The first strophe sets forth the image of God, and the second describes his eschatological action. God is addressed as Lord, God, Savior, and Mighty One. The image is that of the warrior God, an image we have already seen in last week's reading from Zephaniah. "The LORD, your God, is in your midst, a warrior who gives victory" (Zeph. 3:17). As we have seen, this image involves the action of God in the fate of the nation of Israel and its concrete political realities.

This image continues in the second strophe, which deals with the warrior's eschatological action. The metaphor of "strength with his arm" recalls Ps. 89:13: "You have a mighty arm; strong is your hand, high your right hand." This psalm celebrates the eternal covenant with David and how God has given to the king God's power. The opening of the psalm resembles the opening of the Magnificat: "I will sing of your steadfast love, O LORD, forever; with my mouth I will proclaim your faithfulness to all generations" (Ps. 89:1).

The contrasts revolve around the top and the bottom of society, a contrast Jesus made frequently in his parables. While the first strophe paraded titles for the warrior God, the second parades descriptions of a polarized society.

Line 1 (v. 51)	the proud	A
Line 2 (v. 52)	powerful	A
	lowly	B
Line 3 (v. 53)	hungry	B
	rich	A
Line 4 (v. 54)	servant	B

The *AB* pattern creates an asymmetrical interlocking. The "proud" in late Second Temple psalms is frequently a veiled reference to the Romans, and the "lowly" refers to Israel, oppressed by the nations (Deut. 26:7; Ps. 136:23). The hymn makes clear that the salvation which the God Savior brings is the liberation of the nation Israel according to the promises God made to Israel. Jesus' beatitudes pick up on this theme: "Blessed are you who are poor, for yours is the kingdom of God. Blessed are you who are hungry now, for you will be filled" (Luke 6:20-21). The divorce between the spiritual and the secular that characterizes modern thought is foreign to the sensibilities of Israel and early Christianity. Salvation is corporate; it involves all of God's creation. To be in covenant with the God of Israel will have inevitable political implications. The liturgy has held before our eyes for these four Sundays of Advent various scenarios for the end time as a reminder that in Jesus we confess that the end is now. "The Mighty One has done great things for me." "Blessed are you who are poor, for yours *is* the kingdom of God."

The Nativity of Our Lord

Lutheran	Roman Catholic	Episcopal	Revised Common
Isa. 9:2-7	Isa. 9:2-7	Isa. 9:2-4, 6-7	Isa. 9:2-7
Titus 2:11-14	Titus 2:11-14	Titus 2:11-14	Titus 2:11-14
Luke 2:1-20	Luke 2:1-14	Luke 2:1-14	Luke 2:1-14 (15-20)

FIRST LESSON: ISAIAH 9:2-7

Isaiah was active in Jerusalem during the divided monarchy between 740 and 701 B.C.E. His prophecies have proved so polyvalent, so pregnant with meaning and significance, that they have provided later prophets, Judaism, and Christianity an almost inexhaustible source of inspiration.

Today's first reading is preceded by a description of "the people who walked in darkness." They are idolaters who "consult the ghosts and the familiar spirits that chirp and mutter" and their ancestors (8:19). The prophet responds initially: "Surely, those who speak like this will have no dawn!" (8:20), and then reverses the prophecy in favor of hope: "The people who walked in darkness have seen a great light" (9:2). The light is the day of liberation when their oppressor is thrown off. "For the yoke of their burden, and the bar across their shoulders, the rod of their oppressor, you have broken" (9:4). The metaphor of the yoked oxen parallels that of darkness, and release from the yoke symbolizes freedom.

The promise of light is reinforced by the promise of a new, ideal David who will rule with justice and righteousness and establish his throne forever. This ideal David's birth is announced with great names. Some have suggested this hymn was originally part of an enthronement eulogy, perhaps for Josiah or Hezekiah that has been recycled as an eschatological prophecy. Similar exalted epithets occur in Egyptian hymnology. "His title will be: Wonderful Counsellor, Mighty Hero, Eternal Father, Prince of Peace" (9:6, REB). This translation is probably as accurate as one can be; the NRSV "Mighty God" is misleading. This ruler's advice will bring about the people's well-being; he will be a hero-warrior, a father to his people forever, and a prince who brings peace.

All of this will happen because of God's zeal, not because of the people's goodness. God's zeal for justice, righteousness, and peace will bring this ideal king as well as relief for the people walking in darkness.

We can easily see how this prophecy fired the hearts of those in exile, of those in the desert at Qumran, of early Christians, and even now of all those bent under the rod of an oppressor. Although early Christians applied this text to Jesus, an extension of its original meaning, it is also fitting for us to remember David on Christmas, because the notion of a restored Davidic house by which God will be faithful to God's covenant provided one of the primary vehicles for the maintenance of Israel's hope.

SECOND LESSON: TITUS 2:11-14

The second lesson comes from a late first-century baptismal formula in Titus; this reading too is fitting on Christmas because baptism reminds us of our own birth in Christ, when we passed from darkness to light.

The social situation and context of the Pastorals bear directly on their proper interpretation. Written late in the first century, these letters belong to at least the third or fourth generation of Christianity. That they look back to Paul as their hero and address Timothy and Titus, his followers, indicates that the communities of these letters see themselves as belonging to what one may call a Pauline school. They stand in the Pauline tradition but their position is not identical with that of Paul. Paul was concerned with the relation of Christianity to Judaism, the initial questions of identity, and the end of the eschaton. In the Pastorals the eschatological crisis has passed, the identity of the Christian religion is clearly established, and the dominating question is how to relate to the Roman Empire. The communities represented by the Pastorals have increasingly adopted the language and practices of the Empire.

The Roman emperor Domitian (81–96 C.E.) applied to himself the titles "Our Master [or Lord] and our God" as well as "Savior." The phrase "appearance of grace" likewise reflects the imperial cult. Here "grace" is not the grace of God as Paul understood it, but the "gift" of a ruler: by the grace of Caesar such and such occurs. (See Martin Dibelius and Hans Conzelmann, *The Pastoral Epistles*, trans. Philip Buttolph and Adela Yarbro, Hermeneia [Philadelphia: Fortress Press,

1972], 143–44, for extensive references.) This adaptation of Christianity to the hieratic structure of the Roman Empire would continue for some time.

These titles have become central to Christian vocabulary. One can already see the process of adaptation beginning in the Gospel of John, when at the conclusion of the story of Jesus and the Samaritan Woman the villagers confess him as Savior of the world (John 4:42). The contrast between Jesus and the Roman emperor is ironic. In the Pastorals the titles have lost their ironic overtones. Christianity makes a direct claim that conflicts with that of the Roman emperor. What applies to the emperor in all his magnificence applies even more to Jesus.

This process of adaptation occurred not only with christological titles but also with household codes to prescribe Christian ethics. The REB nicely catches the sloganeering of Titus 2:12: "to live a life of temperance, honesty, and godliness in the present age." This description of the Christian life is nearly identical with "the ideal of Greek ethics" (see Dibelius and Conzelmann, *Pastoral Epistles*, 142). Temperance, honesty (NRSV, "upright"), and godliness (NAB, "devoutly") are three of the four cardinal virtues. Only courage is missing. The Christian is to be trained (REB, "disciplined") in a similar way to the philosophical practice of Hellenistic society.

The Pastorals raise the critical question of how far the Christian community can adapt to the standards of the surrounding culture. This question has dogged Christianity since its earliest days and lies behind Paul's debate with the Corinthians as well as his break with Peter. With their wholesale adaptation of the imperial cult to the new religion, the Pastorals represent an extreme in the New Testament on this issue. Today, when the economic culture of capitalism has almost totally overrun the religious values of Christmas, we need to ask, How far do we go? Did the Pastorals go too far or do they perhaps represent the limit?

GOSPEL: LUKE 2:1-20

Only two of the four canonical Gospels have birth narratives. Mark begins his Gospel with the preaching of John the Baptist, and John begins with a hymn celebrating the preexistence of the Word. Matthew's birth narrative describes events before and after the birth, though not the birth itself. But Luke narrates the birth and the signs of its manifestation. The two stories in Matthew and Luke are hardly reconcilable, and efforts to do so only distort the integrity of each story.

The Lukan narrative has three main parts: the setting (2:1-5), the birth (6-7), and the manifestation (8-20). The manifestation is divided into two parts, first the angel's appearance (8-14), then the reaction to the manifestation (15-20). The story begins with a decree *going out* from the mighty Augustus and ends with the shepherds *returning*, glorifying and praising God. Thus the story is surrounded by an implied motion of expansion and contraction.

Luke introduces Jesus' birth story with the Emperor Augustus's proclamation of a worldwide census. Augustus casts a wide shadow across this birth narrative. The adopted son of Julius Caesar, Octavian (Augustus) defeated Mark Antony and Cleopatra at Actium in 31 B.C.E., ushering in an era of peace after a long period of civil war. This era of peace was celebrated throughout the Roman Empire. The reign of Augustus was described as an eschatological age of peace and salvation brought to humankind by the divine Augustus. The poet Virgil celebrated this imperial eschatology both in his *Aeneid* and in the *Fourth Eclogue* of his *Georgics*. The latter announced the birth of Augustus in such a messianic way that Christians later adopted it as a prophecy for the birth of Jesus.

> Now is come the last age of the son of Cumae; the great line of the centuries begins anew. Now the Virgin returns, the reign of Saturn returns; now a new generation descends from heaven on high. Only do thou, pure Lucina, smile on the birth of the child, under whom the iron brood shall first cease, and a golden race spring up throughout the world! Thine own Apollo now is king!

Luke may have been the first to link the birth of Jesus with the reign of Augustus, but he was not the last. The early Christian fathers were fond of such a linkage. Melito of Sardis (2nd century) emphasized the providential development of the empire and the church and Origen (3rd century) maintained that the Augustan peace was ordained by God to spread Christianity. Although the church fathers saw the relation between the empire and the birth of Jesus in positive terms, Luke's presentation emphasizes the contrasts in that relation.

Luke's vehicle for drawing Jesus and Augustus onto the same stage was the universal census. This census not only demonstrates the arbitrary and autocratic power of Augustus to force peoples to do his bidding, but also provides Luke with a means to locate Jesus in Bethlehem, where tradition and prophecy record his birth. Matthew and Luke view differently Jesus' relation to Bethlehem. For Matthew Jesus' hometown is Bethlehem, where he is born in a house (Matt. 2:11). Matthew must get Jesus from Bethlehem to Nazareth, the Galilean city associated with his ministry. By contrast, Luke views Jesus as a Galilean from Nazareth and so must get Mary and Joseph to Bethlehem for his birth. The census serves this function. Unfortunately no historical evidence exists to support this census, although many scholars have tried in vain to defend the Lukan account. Joseph Fitzmyer seems to offer the best summary of the evidence: Luke "indulged in some rhetoric in his desire to locate the birth of Jesus in Bethlehem under . . . Caesar Augustus" (Fitzmyer, *Luke,* 1:400).

The account contrasts sharply the birth of Jesus with the power of Augustus. The description is cleverly laid out, with the explanatory point made last. After mentioning people with power—Emperor Augustus and Quirinius, the governor of Syria, the province to which Galilee and Judaea belonged—Luke states that Joseph proceeded to Bethlehem, "because he was of the house of David by descent" (2:4, REB). This linking of names (Augustus, Quirinius, David) creates an expectation of power, imperial power. Mary gives birth to a son, her firstborn, which implies a special status under Mosaic law (Exod. 13:2). She next wraps him in cloth bands, which was the normal practice (Wisd. 7:4; Ezek. 16:4). But then she lays him in a manger, the trough from which animals eat. Now the account has taken a turn for which the narrator has not prepared the reader. This surprising effect is almost totally lost on moderns because we know the story so well and have romanticized and combined it with Matthew. The last line of the birth's description reinforces this loss of expected status: "because there was no place for them in the inn" (2:7). A story that had begun with Augustus and mentioned King David ends with a newborn laid to rest in the animals' trough because there was no room for his parents in the inn. One can hardly imagine greater contrast between the power and status of the emperor and the status of the newborn.

The narrative shifts to the manifestation of the birth and continues along this same line of loss of status. It follows basically the form of an announcement story. The manifestation of the birth is to shepherds. On the one hand, shepherds are appropriate recipients of the message, since David himself was a shepherd. On the other hand, by rabbinic standards shepherds are unclean, because they do not observe set borders, but follow their sheep wherever they go. Like the publican in the parable (Luke 18:9-14), they are appropriate recipients of the message of salvation because they are poor and unclean. The angel echoes Isa. 61:1, which Jesus reads when he inaugurates his ministry at Nazareth: "He has anointed me to bring good news to the poor . . . to proclaim the year of the Lord's favor" (Luke 4:18-19).

The angel's announcement is a summary of Lukan Christology: "I am bringing you good news of great joy for all the people: to you is born this day in the city of David a Savior, who is the Messiah, the Lord" (2:10-11). The angel "preaches the gospel" (*euangelizomai*). Luke never uses the noun "good news" (*euangelion*) but always the verb. The gospel is not a concept but an action of liberation, as Isa. 61:1 makes clear. Of the titles the angel uses, two are distinctly Jewish and two belong to the emperor's cult. "David" and "Messiah" are closely associated because David is the archetype of the Messiah. Yet this birth narrative stands in sharp contrast to the expectations of a Davidic Messiah. How could such a one "restore the kingdom to Israel" (Acts 1:6)? The same goes for the titles "Savior" and "Lord" (*kyrios*). These two are prominent in the cult of Augustus, whose birthday was proclaimed as "good news." This child from the house of David seems to be no match for one from the house of Caesar.

After the angel's message, the sky is filled with angels praising God and singing an anthem. The last line of their anthem has a well-known textual problem that concerns the Greek word meaning "goodwill" or "favor." In the best manuscripts the reading is a genitive, while the *textus receptus*, which Luther and the KJV translators followed, reads the nominative. The latter produces the translation "on earth peace, good will toward men" (KJV). Modern translations prefer the genitive reading, which leads to the translation "on earth peace among those whom he favors." This reading produces a nice balance, which is characteristic of Second Temple hymns.

Glory	*in the highest heaven*	to <u>God</u>
and *upon the earth*	**peace**	<u>among those peoples whom he favors.</u>

The first line has the pattern A *B* <u>C</u> while the second has *B*A<u>C</u>, producing a chiasm between the A*B* elements.

The chief sign of the reign of this new Messiah baby is peace, which also happens to be the chief sign of the age of Augustus, celebrated in the empire's official propaganda. Frederick Danker quotes an inscription commemorating the celebration of Augustus's birth that makes this point.

> Providence, that orders everything in our lives, has displayed extraordinary concern and compassion and crowned our life with perfection itself. She has brought into the world Augustus and filled him with distinguished goodness for the benefit of humanity. In her beneficence she has granted us and those who will come after us [a Savior] who has made war to cease and who shall order all things well. The [epiphany] of Caesar transcends the expectations of [all who anticipated the good news.] Not only has he outstripped all benefactors who have gone before him, but he will leave posterity no hope of surpassing him. The birth date of our God has signaled the beginning of good news for the world. (*Jesus and the New Age: A Commentary on St. Luke's Gospel*, rev. ed. [Philadelphia: Fortress Press, 1988], 54)

Luke contrasts not only the status of Augustus with that of the new Messiah, but also the peace that they bring. In Judaism and in early Christianity "peace" denoted the wholeness, the completeness, that comes when one's life corresponds to the will of God. In such a wholeness the proper relation between God and humans, humans and nature, and human and human is restored. This peace gives glory to God and heals the division between the highest and the lowest. All is one in God. Thus it is not a peace or stability built on the backs of the poor and slaves as was the Roman Empire, but a peace that announces liberation to the poor, the slave, the outcast.

We do not know the details of Jesus' birth. The birth narratives tell us nothing concrete about his birth. They are meditations on the significance of that birth from the point of view of the outcome of his life, death, and resurrection. It is perhaps fitting that the details are missing, that the Messiah slipped into the world unnoticed, hidden away. This is precisely how God almost always appears in the world, in ways that would scandalize us and seem most inappropriate, despite the advertisements for the so-called great deeds. Thus in spite of the evangelist's efforts to draw the sharpest contrast with Augustus, somehow in our imagination we always insist that Jesus was nevertheless greater than Augustus, that he could have been born in a palace had he so desired. Perhaps, but for Luke such a Jesus would not have been the Messiah.

Christmas Day

Lutheran	Roman Catholic	Episcopal	Revised Common
Isa. 52:7-10	Isa. 52:7-10	Isa. 52:7-10	Isa. 52:7-10
Heb. 1:1-9	Heb. 1:1-6	Heb. 1:1-12	Heb. 1:14 (5-12)
John 1:1-14	John 1:1-18	John 1:1-14	John 1:1-14

FIRST LESSON: ISAIAH 52:7-10

The first reading belongs to a prayer that poses one of the perennial Judeo-Christian problems: When evil surrounds us, does it mean that God has abandoned us? Even though in the Hebrew understanding creation is good, humanity has sinned, so has God abandoned creation? This problem became acute around 540 B.C.E., when Cyrus II of Persia was attacking the Babylonian Empire. These songs belong to the exilic period and were written by a prophet different from the one who composed chapters 1-39 of Isaiah. The section comprising chapters 40–66 is frequently referred to as Deutero-Isaiah.

Isaiah 52:7-10 belongs to a larger unit that extends from 51:9 through 52:12. On both sides of this unit are Songs of the Suffering Servant. Three imperatives provide a minimal structure for the unit. The first addresses the Lord: "Awake, awake, put on strength, O arm of the LORD" (51:9). The next two address Jerusalem, with the third employing the same imperatives as the first: "Rouse yourself, rouse yourself! Stand up, O Jerusalem" (51:17); "Awake, awake, put on your strength, O Zion!" (52:1). Many debate the form of this section: Some argue against any recognizable pattern, while others notice the similarity with the psalms of lamentation (e.g., Psalms 44, 74). Just as God acted victoriously in creation and the exodus, so too will God act now. "Awake, as in the days of old, the generations of long ago! . . . Was it not you who dried up the sea, the waters of the great deep; who made the depths of the sea a way for the redeemed to cross over?" (Isa. 51:9, 11).

The first lesson comes from the lamentation's last part, which proclaims God's eschatological deliverance of Jerusalem. The point of view is that of sentries who spy Yahweh approaching, announcing peace and the good news of salvation. The LXX employs several terms that will become key in early Christianity: *euangelizomai* (to announce the good news), *sōtēria* (salvation), and *basileusei* (he [God] rules). Neither the vocabulary of Israel nor that of early Christianity uses these as "spiritual" terms, without concrete reference. They are not Docetic, although Christians have frequently so used them. "Salvation" and "the rule of God" refer to the concrete world of humans, to political realities. The Lord "has redeemed Jerusalem. The LORD has bared his holy arm in the sight of all nations, and the whole world from end to end shall see the deliverance [salvation— NRSV, NAB] wrought by our God" (52:9-10, REB). Salvation (deliverance) means Jerusalem's restoration. The salvation of God is a public act, not private or personal.

This view runs counter to the individualism that characterizes American piety as well as our notions of separation of church and state. We are more comfortable with a personal, private God than a God who acts publicly. Yet the Judeo-Christian claim that God acts in history demands that we think seriously about this issue, especially at Christmastime when the commercialization of God's act threatens to undermine the very values for which Jesus' birth stands. Forty percent of all retail goods are sold during the four weeks between Thanksgiving and Christmas Day. As Richard Horsley has pointed out, "the Christmas story has clearly come to have a material significance: it helps to legitimate the festival of retailing and consumption of goods" (*The Liberation of Christmas: The Infancy Narratives in Social Context* [New York: Crossroad, 1989], ix). Perhaps the prophet would today spot Yahweh coming not as the deliverer but as an avenger for our spoiling of creation.

SECOND LESSON: HEBREWS 1:1-6

The first four verses of the Epistle to the Hebrews are a single sentence of a rather complex form greatly favored by artistic and rhetorical Greek prose. It indicates the high standards of this letter. Yet for translators it poses considerable problems since modern English favors short sentences. The KJV translated all four verses as a single sentence in magnificent Elizabethan prose: "God, who at sundry times and in divers manners spake in time past unto the fathers by the prophets, hath in these last days spoken unto us by his Son. . . ."

This initial sentence has three parts in balanced clauses. What follows is an effort to indicate the form based on the translation of Harold

41

Attridge (*The Epistle to the Hebrews*, Hermeneia [Philadelphia: Fortress Press, 1989], 35).

Part 1

a (1) Having spoken of old in multiple forms and multiple fashions to the fathers through the prophets,

b (2) in these final days God has spoken to us through a Son,

c whom he established as heir of all things,

d through whom he also created the universe,

Part 2

a (3) who, being the radiance of his glory and the imprint of his fundamental reality,

b bearing all things by his powerful word,

c having made purification for sins,

d took a seat at the right hand of the Majesty on high,

Part 3

(4) having become as far superior to the angels as he has inherited a name more excellent than they.

In form this first sentence of Hebrews is an exordium, a formal opening of an argument that summarizes the main points to be made; and this exordium does present in a nutshell the letter's major themes.

Part 1 consists of four lines, with the first line in Greek dominated by an alliteration of *p* sounds, something impossible to reproduce in an English translation. This first part establishes the difference between God's speech or word in former times as compared with that speech in God's Son. The contrast between the present and the past, the old and the new, has nothing to do with the truth or completeness of God's word in the past. God's speech in the past was disjointed. The NRSV has "in many and various ways" while the NAB has "in partial and various ways." "Partial" is misleading because nothing has been left out; God has communicated in varied and multiform ways through the prophets. Such diversity contrasts with the present communication in God's Son. Jesus' divine sonship dominates the letter's Christology, as we will shortly see. The present is also "the final days," an apocalyptic term for the end times. This phrase reminds us that early Christian expectation on this point differs from our own; for the author of Hebrews history has come to its conclusion in Jesus.

The *c* and *d* lines of part 1 first describe the son as the "heir of all things." "Heir" is one of the primary senses of "son" in the ancient world. For example, the parable of the Prodigal Son says a man has two sons (Luke 15:11), meaning that he has two heirs. The inheritance provides the story's narrative tension. An heir receives the inheritance after the father's death, so "heir" symbolizes the end of creation when the Son will receive all. Line *d* looks to the other end of creation and makes the Son the one through whom God also created the universe. The Greek word translated as "universe" (NAB, REB) or "worlds" (NRSV) means in its primary sense "the ages" (*aiōnas*). The narrator views the world in its temporal sense, as the sphere of history. The Son is the active agent both at the beginning and the end of history, or as the book of Revelation puts it, the Alpha and Omega (Rev. 22:13).

Part 2 (v. 3) is probably a fragment of an early Christian hymn that the author has reworked to fit the exordium. It has the form of other such hymnic fragments (for example, Phil. 2:6-11 or Col. 1:15-18). All these hymns derive from the Jewish wisdom tradition, with its highly syncretistic tendencies. The high Christology that typifies these hymns probably first emerged in this hymnic tradition.

Line *a* describes how the Son is like God. He is the radiance of God's glory. In the Judaic tradition, "glory" designates the divine reality: God is glory. The word translated "radiance" can have either an active sense, refulgence (NAB), or a passive sense, reflection (NRSV). It can be the light that the mirror reflects or the mirror itself. Which sense one should prefer is not clear; perhaps both are intended, as is possible in poetry. That the Son is the "imprint of his fundamental reality" parallels "radiance of his glory." Just as the signet ring stands for the master's authority and presence, so also is the Son the Father's stamp (REB).

Lines *b* and *c* denote the Son's activity. Not only was everything created through him, but he also sustains its being. Even more, he purified us from sins. For the author of Hebrews this is Jesus' essential activity. It recalls his priestly work of being the perfect sacrifice that puts an end to all sacrifices. The required repetition of previous sacrificial offerings underlines their imperfection and incompleteness. They remind us of sin but do not cleanse, as does the Son's voluntary death.

Line *d* culminates in the Son's exaltation to the right hand of God. The exaltation motif derives its language from Ps. 110:1. The high priest who offers the perfect sacrifice and his exaltation are key symbols in the theology of Hebrews, while Psalm 110 plays a prominent role in both the structure of the letter and its way of thinking. The language of exaltation comes ultimately from the court practice of the ancient world. For the king to raise someone to his right hand was to give that person the same honor and status as the king. Exaltation, like resurrection, is another metaphor that comes from the experience of rising from sleep and is used to explain God's activity in Jesus.

Part 3 (v. 4) closes the exordium with a celebration of the Son's exaltation. The name that he receives at the exaltation is "more excellent" than the angels. The theme of "more excellent than the angels" leads into the collection of proof texts with which the argument proper begins (1:5-14). Thus this last part serves both to conclude the exordium and to introduce the letter's first part.

For many Christians, Christmas is the apex of the liturgical year. It has become *the* feast, the one that draws the most people to church. Many liturgists decry this development, insisting instead that Easter deserves this role. Although from the point of view of tradition, Easter is surely preeminent, one can understand why a capitalist consumer society needs such a liturgical celebration as Christmas has become. It is that one time of the year in which we experience a sense of new life, of rebirth. We experience ourselves and others as we wish to experience them every day—as innocent. We experience a sense of innocence and unity with others because of the giving, regardless of how exploited that giving is. To give, as Scrooge discovered, is to live beyond oneself, to acknowledge the other as more important than we are, or as a theologian would say, to experience a transcendental moment. That sense of innocence and unity is what the author to Hebrews is describing in the exordium. Jesus unifies all of creation in his purification of us and in his exaltation, whereby the bridge between God and us is overcome by a free gift of God.

GOSPEL: JOHN 1:1-18

The prologue to the Fourth Gospel is a consummate work of art, ranking among the world's great poetry. I make this statement not just as an accolade but to indicate an important consideration for the poem's interpretation. As poetry its intention is not primarily philosophical or even theological. Like all art, poetry seeks to enable the reader to experience a reality that goes beyond the daily and mundane, the somnambulistic sphere in which we move about as if in a dream. Poetry intensifies language, puts it in the crucible of metaphor, to expose us to something new and different.

The author of this masterpiece is anonymous. The hymn's author and the author of the Gospel are probably not the same person. While the hymn makes an adequate summary of the Gospel, some of its vocabulary and concepts do not appear in the Gospel. For example, the hymn is about the Word, but this usage never occurs in the Gospel proper. Furthermore, this Gospel has undergone at least two editions. The original Gospel ended obviously at 20:30-31. The resurrection stories of chapter 21 differ from those of chapter 20, and the editor has reworked the original ending in 21:25. (See Raymond Brown, *The Community of the Beloved Disciple: The Life, Loves, and Hates of an Individual Church in New Testament Times* [New York: Paulist, 1979].) Most scholars believe the prologue hymn was added to the Gospel in the course of its second edition. Thus we must imagine a more complex process in the formation of this Gospel than we have traditionally imagined.

The poem or hymn divides into three parts with two prose interludes that concern John the Baptist, always referred to in the Fourth Gospel as John. The first part (vv. 1-5) has as its theme the Word acting with God; the second (9-14) concerns the Word's encounter with the world; while the third (15-18) forms a confession to the Word.

The prologue has two separate types of motion, which add to its aesthetic impression. Although throughout the hymn the language is poetical and highly metaphorical, the language does shift. The first part has a cosmic, quasi-philosophical and even mythical cast. Some object to the term *mythical*, but it well describes how this language functions. Myth was one of the few ways the ancients (and likewise we moderns) had to speak of such realities, since one cannot describe them literally. The hymn's second part shifts gradually from the cosmic-mythical language of light to the realization that the hymn is now speaking about someone, a historical being, the Word made flesh. The hymn's third part shifts again, to the language of confession.

A second type of motion in the hymn is interwoven with the first. One might call this motion vertical: from before creation to creation, to conflict and incarnation, and finally to witness. The first type of motion gives the hymn its special poetic aura, while the second provides it with a strong narrative drive.

Much has been written about the hymn's background in an effort to find the key that will render it totally intelligible. The hymn draws on many different strands of Mediterranean religion, especially Jewish wisdom. But no one strand furnishes the complete explanation. Like the other New Testament christological hymns, the prologue is a special blend of the syncretistic currents in the Mediterranean world, Christian faith, and liturgical confession.

The hymn opens with a wordplay on the LXX version of the book of Genesis, "In the beginning" (*en archē*). The temporal indicators are different, however; the hymn begins before the beginning, so to speak. The Word is the first step, creation the second.

The translation of *logos* as "word" has long been traditional and nothing is wrong with it, but one may still ask why the author chose this metaphor as the dominating one for understanding Jesus. Here scholars usually bring in the matter of background. Some point to Philo, who speaks of the Logos as the mediating agent between God and creation. This use indicates that God had become so transcendent or hierarchical that he needed a mediator. But the hymn in John runs contrary to this understanding of God, since the Word is not just a mediator but becomes a human! Others point to Wisdom, and Wisdom speculation has undoubtedly influenced the hymn. But again, why did the author not use the term for "Wisdom"?

The clue lies, I think, in the poetic possibilities of *logos*. "Word" in English has an abstract, almost reified sense, whereas in both Greek and Hebrew it has a much more dynamic sense. The first sense of *logos* (and Hebrew *dābār*) is "speaking." This sense is clear in the Genesis creation story: the word of God brings the world into being. The hymn undoubtedly alludes to this Genesis story. Thus one could translate the first three clauses of the hymn: "In the beginning was speaking, and the speaking was to God, and the speaking was divine (or God)." In the hymn's poetic vision God is speech, and in the logic of the metaphor of speech, one speaks to someone. Thus God is a mutual conversation, God speaking to himself (herself, itself). From the hymn's point of view God is essentially incarnational, oriented to speaking with someone. In this sense the hymn pictures God's relentless drive to carry on a conversation. God is not alone but a voice in search of a conversation.

The primary understanding of God as speech explains why God's Speech creates. Based on the simple observation that the dead do not speak and that life is light (i.e., sun and warmth), one can say that speech is life. Thus the bridges between these images explain not only the creative act but the divine sustenance of all life. But light has an opponent: darkness. Again, the theme of light and darkness, though widespread in the ancient Mediterranean world, finds its clearest echo in Genesis. While darkness, the opposite of light, is named, the opposites of life and Speech are not. The implication is that for God to be silent would be for God to be dead.

After introducing John as one sent by God, the first interlude states firmly that he is not the light. One should not brush aside this interlude as an editorial problem or addition. It represents the poetic interweaving of the cosmic-mythic and historical, thus imitating the incarnation itself. These jarring shifts between different worlds are part of the hymn's poetic effect that help the hearer anticipate the incarnation.

The hymn's second part describes the incarnation, not from a linear but from an impressionistic perspective. A literalist mind-set leads some scholars to posit two different types of incarnation in the hymn, but this is not necessary. Writing poetry, the author can set aside the time sequence in favor of an impressionistic view of the incarnation.

Light is the dominant metaphor in this second part. But verse 10 intends a personal view of the light. In the Greek the personal pronouns are "he," not "it" as would be the case if "light" were the antecedent. From "the world" and from "his own" (both terms probably refer to the same group) he meets rejection. They do not recognize him. The world does not recognize that it is "from God." They choose darkness, not light; death, not life; silence, not speech. But to all who do accept him, he gives them the right (NEB) to be children of God. These "were born not by natural generation nor by human choice nor by a man's decision but of God" (13, NAB). This same radical understanding of rebirth forms the basis of the Nicodemus speech in chapter 3. Those who accept him understand that they are really "of God."

"And the Speech became flesh." In the context of this poem this statement does not indicate a sequence—the poem has already described the incarnation. Rather, the poem shifts back to its primary metaphor, Speech or Word, and describes its total humanization. Nowhere does Jewish Wisdom speculation imagine the enfleshment of Wisdom, and in gnostic speculation such a scene is a tragedy. The Speech of God has come full circle. Not only is it God's agent at creation, but now it becomes itself a creature. Such total identification of God and creation threatens to obliterate the line between the two. The next line reemphasizes the thought by noting literally that "he built his tent among us." "Tent" is a common Hellenistic metaphor for human life (hence "lived among us," NRSV; "home," REB) and also harks back to the exodus image of God's tent that traveled with Israel.

When one senses the radicalness of the hymn's claim, momentous theological questions arise. Does the incarnation mean that the goal of human existence is that we should become divinized, as Greek Orthodox Christianity has insisted, or does it mean that God became humanized, like us? While one can find in the Fourth Gospel evidence for both positions, the weight would seem to fall on the humanization of God. That is the point in the resurrection story involving Thomas. The resurrected Christ demonstrates his very fleshliness and Thomas confesses him as Lord and God. This issue has important implications for how we view our life. If we are to strive after divinization, then we must strive to be God-like and become the community of the perfect. Life on earth becomes a "vale of tears," and we should escape behind iconostasis; in heaven we will find our true vocation. But if God has become like us, then God accepts us as we are and becomes *sympatico* with us. The gap between God and humanity no longer exists, and we have a powerful warrant to overcome all other gaps in human life.

The incarnation precipitates another shift in the hymn, a change in voice from third person to first person, "we." At the moment of incarnation the narrator and hearer are fused into a confessing community of those who have seen the glory of the Word, the essence of God—Speech in flesh.

The second interlude jumps ahead to the Gospel narrative, again distorting the hymn's time frame. In the hymn's third part the confession generated by the incarnation continues. It concludes with the ultimate paradox that no one has seen God except the Son who is God. Thus the Father makes the Son known so that we can see God. We will see God only in the incarnation, that is, in flesh.

Both Hebrews and this Gospel remind us that the fundamental Christian claim is that in Jesus God has brought creation and history to its completion. Christmas is not the celebration of a beginning, but the beginning of the end, a new birth, a rebirth. Christmas and Easter are the same feast. The sense of otherness and innocence, of goodwill and peace, are the eschatological presents that this newness of life offers. Just as these early Christian hymns had to be incorporated into the larger story of Jesus even at the risk of distorting the sense of time, so also we must integrate the Christmas story into our life. The Speech must become flesh. That integration will produce a distortion in the logic of our everyday life called the fullness of grace. We have seen his glory, we have experienced his birth on this Christmas day.

First Sunday after Christmas

Lutheran	Roman Catholic	Episcopal	Revised Common
Jer. 31:10-13	1 Sam. 1:20-22, 24-28	Isa. 61:10—62:3	1 Sam. 2:18-20, 26
Heb. 2:10-18	1 John 3:1-2, 21-24	Gal. 3:23-25; 4:4-7	Col. 3:12-17
Luke 2:41-52	Luke 2:41-52	John 1:1-18	Luke 2:41-52

FIRST LESSON: ISAIAH 61:10—62:3; JEREMIAH 31:10-13; 1 SAMUEL 1:20-22, 24-28; 2:18-20, 26

The lectionary assignments for both the first and second readings vary widely for this First Sunday after Christmas. The readings from Jeremiah and Isaiah are similar. They are both hymns from the postexilic period celebrating Yahweh's redemption of Israel. We have dealt with these types of hymns in the Advent readings. The women dancing in the street and the dressing bride awaiting her beloved are images that exhibit the love and the joy associated with Israel's anticipation of its beloved God. In the post-Christmas period these two readings serve to remind us of the intimate connection between Yahweh's promises made to Israel and those made in Christ. If we confess that Jesus is the Messiah, then we confess that he is the fulfillment of Israel's promises. A supersessionist theology that vacates the promises made to Israel runs the risk of vacating its own promises.

The other two readings from First Samuel relate aspects of the Samuel story that parallel the Gospel reading of Jesus in the Temple. These readings probably also indicate the inspiration for the Jesus story. Samuel's birth too was a miraculous event for Hannah, who had been barren. She bargained with the Lord, promising that if he would grant her a son, she would dedicate him to the Lord. In due time, a child was born to Hannah and she named him Samuel, which means "I have asked him of the LORD" (1 Sam. 1:20). Faithful to her promise, she enrolled him in the Lord's service at the temple in Shiloh. Through Samuel the line of the judges was destined to continue, for "the boy Samuel continued to grow both in stature and in favor with the LORD and with the people" (2:26).

49

SECOND LESSON: GALATIANS 3:23-25; 4:4-7; COLOSSIANS 3:12-17; HEBREWS 2:10-18; 1 JOHN 3:1-2, 21-24

The diverse second readings all share the common theme of humanity's unity through the fatherhood of God. In the context of the first century C.E., these claims of unity competed with the propaganda of the Roman Empire that insisted that the Roman imperium was the best basis for unity and peace. The logic of the early Christian claim rests first on the commonality of Jesus with us. "For the one who sanctifies and those who are sanctified all have one Father. For this reason Jesus is not ashamed to call them brothers and sisters" (Heb. 2:11). In Galatians Paul makes a similar claim when he notes that the law was a disciplinarian but "in Christ Jesus you are all children of God through faith" (Gal. 3:26). Jesus' solidarity with us has to do with God's appointment of Jesus and our divine paternity. "See what love the Father has given us, that we should be called children of God; and that is what we are. . . . And this is his commandment, that we should believe in the name of his Son Jesus Christ and love one another, just as he has commanded us" (1 John 3:1, 23). As the Pauline quotation implies and First John makes explicit, the bond among God, Jesus, and ourselves is love. "Above all, clothe yourselves with love, which binds everything together in perfect harmony" (Col. 3:14). The bonding in love contrasts with the bonding of diverse people in the Roman Empire through imperium, through power and might.

We live in an age that has powerful drives toward both unity and division. The electronic revolution is quickly producing a global village. More and more of the world is interconnected. No longer are we divided by two great superpowers. Yet at the same time ethnic tensions threaten to sunder the global village into collections of warring tribes. All of this is based on power and claims to power. The world seems divided into oppressors and victims, each claiming their own power. The Christian vision of unity is the antithesis of this power orientation; Christian unity is based on love, a love that results from redemption.

GOSPEL: LUKE 2:41-52

Today's Gospel reading about Jesus in the Temple when he was twelve is unique in the canonical Gospel traditions. Only Luke shows the slightest interest in Jesus' youth, although this theme flourished in the later elaboration of the Jesus tradition. The *Infancy Gospel of Thomas* (earliest attestation 183 C.E.) contains many such stories, including one clearly dependent on the Lukan narrative. A comparison of the two stories is instructive because the former more strongly accents the youth's power and astonishing intelligence. The *Infancy Gospel of Thomas* version initially follows the Lukan story closely, but diverges at the description of Jesus' performance before the teachers. "Everyone paid attention to him and all were amazed how, though a child, he was able to silence the elders and teachers of the people, interpreting the main points of the Law and the enigmatic sayings of the prophets" (*Infancy Gospel of Thomas* 19:4-5; Robert J. Miller, ed., *The Complete Gospels* [Sonoma, Calif.: Polebridge, 1992], 371). When Mary questions the youth, the teachers and Pharisees exclaim, "You of all women are to be congratulated because God has blessed the fruit of your womb. For we have never seen nor heard of such glory or such virtue and wisdom" (19:10; *Complete Gospels*, 372). By comparison, the interests of the Lukan story are quite modest.

Such tales about the precocious signs exhibited by the great men of antiquity were common. The story Plutarch relates of Alexander's performance before the Persian envoys in his father Philip's court is typical:

> He [Alexander] once entertained the envoys from the Persian king who came during Philip's absence, and associated with them freely. He won upon them by his friendliness, and by asking no childish or trivial questions, but by inquiring about the length of the roads and the character of the journey into the interior, about the king himself, what sort of a warrior he was, and what about the prowess and might of the Persians. The envoys were therefore astonished and regarded the much-talked-of ability of Philip as nothing compared with his son's eager disposition to do great things. (Vernon Robbins, ed., *Ancient Quotes & Anecdotes: From Crib to Crypt*, Foundations and Facets [Sonoma, Calif.: Polebridge, 1989], 33).

Josephus, a famous Jewish historian of the first century C.E., even tells such a tale about himself. "While still a mere boy, about fourteen years old, I won universal applause for my love of letters; insomuch that the chief priests and the leading men of the city [Jerusalem] used constantly to come to me for precise information on some particular in our ordinances" (Josephus *Life* 9, in *Josephus*, trans. H. St. J. Thackeray, Loeb Classical Library [Cambridge, Mass.: Harvard Univ. Press; London: Heinemann, 1926, reprinted 1956], 1:5).

Thus the Jesus story belongs clearly to a group of conventional legends that form part of the common lore of folktales about great men. These legends are based on the common assumption that such a great life must have been prefigured in youth. Stories about George Washington and the cherry tree demonstrate the continuing and abiding power of such stories, even for us moderns. We should treat the Jesus story in the same way. It is a legend showing that Jesus' youth was of interest to the common folk late in the first century. The interest would flower in the second century and later in the infancy gospels with many more exaggerated tales originating in popular piety.

While the story belongs to a popular type, it also shows the specifics of its Christian development. The tale alludes to the story of Hannah and Samuel, whose birth was likewise miraculous. Hannah and her husband went each year to the temple at Shiloh, just as Jesus' parents went to Jerusalem each year for Passover (Luke 2:41); and the reference to Jesus growing in stature and wisdom (2:52) echoes the similar conclusion to the Samuel story (see above). Thus the Hannah/Samuel story provides a type of frame for the Jesus story.

This Jesus story also evidences the strong influence of the pronouncement story, a common form in the Jesus tradition. In a pronouncement story, a saying of Jesus becomes the focus around which a story is developed, so that the situation or setting is almost always secondary to the saying. This form, called in Greek a *chreia*, was a primary means for preserving the oral tradition in writing. It is how the tradition got its written body.

Verse 49 is surely such a pronouncement and, stripped of its setting in the youth of Jesus, could come from almost any period of his ministry. The exact translation of the pronouncement is debated and unresolved. Most modern translations opt for "Did you not know that I must be in my Father's house?" (or "be about my Father's interests"). Either translation is possible, and each has the support of ancient tradition. The Greek text reads literally, "in [or among] the things of my Father it is necessary for me to be." Regardless of how one specifies "the things of my Father," the essential point of the pronouncement is the necessity of identifying "the things of the Father" with Jesus. Thus this first direct speech of Jesus reported in the third Gospel becomes both a summary of his mission and the Gospel's Christology. It alerts the reader to what Jesus will do and by implication who he is.

The story functions as a rounding off and a conclusion to the Lukan birth narratives. This cycle of stories began in the Temple with Zechariah and it ends in the Temple with Jesus. The Gospel itself ends with another Temple reference. The disciples "spent all their time in the temple praising God" (Luke 24:53, REB). Given the centrality of the trip to Jerusalem (temple) in Luke's Gospel, the so-called travel narrative (9:51—19:28), this closure with Jerusalem provides a basic structuring clue: Jerusalem occupies the narrative center of Luke's Gospel.

The story has a triple conclusion. The first brings the tale itself to a close. Jesus goes back to Nazareth with his parents and "was obedient to them" (2:51). The story pictures Jesus as being extraordinary but also abiding by normal childhood constraints. The second conclusion refers to Mary, who "treasured up all these things in her heart" (2:51, REB), which refers to the similar narrator's note ending the birth narrative (2:19). Finally, the conclusion echoes 1 Sam. 2:26: "As Jesus grew he advanced in wisdom and in favour with God and men" (Luke 2:52, REB). It also rephrases the conclusion of Jesus' presentation in the Temple (2:40) and sets the stage for the narrative's next advance.

Mary is more prominent in Luke's Gospel than in any other. This particular story adds some intriguing details to Luke's portrait of her. Many scholars have noted that Mary addresses Jesus by saying, "Your father and I" (2:48), which suggests that this story comes from a segment of the tradition that does not know the virgin birth. The parallel to this story in the *Infancy Gospel of Thomas* avoids this problem by having Mary say, "Why did you do this to us, child?" (19:6). But Luke makes no effort to bring these two traditions into agreement. He pictures Mary as startled and uncomprehending, even offended at Jesus' behavior. Some see this reaction as a reference back to the similar reaction of Jesus' parents to the Simeon prophecy (2:33). At any rate, Luke pictures Mary, like the rest of the disciples, as initially disbelieving (18:34). She comes to faith only gradually and the source of her faith is the same as for the disciples. Luke mentions her among the believers in the upper room after the resurrection (Acts 1:14).

These inconsistencies in Luke's story are instructive. He does not allow some orthodoxy to rewrite the story, and the inconsistencies indicate that he clearly understands the tale's legendary type. He focuses on the pronouncement. The things of the Father are of the essence; the rest can be set aside. These days after Christmas, when we are surrounded by the peripherals of life that have a way of greatly disappointing us, might be an advantageous time to ask what are the things of God.

The Name of Jesus (January 1)

Lutheran	Roman Catholic	Episcopal	Revised Common
Num. 6:22-27	Num. 6:22-27	Exod. 34:1-8	Num. 6:22-27
Rom. 1:1-7 *or* Phil. 2:9-13	Gal. 4:4-7	Rom. 1:1-7	Gal. 4:4-7 *or* Phil. 2:5-11
Luke 2:21	Luke 2:16-21	Luke 2:15-21	Luke 2:15-21

FIRST LESSON: NUMBERS 6:22-27

The lesson from Numbers preserves what is probably one of the oldest sections of the Hebrew Bible and also a summary of the Hebrew faith in Yahweh. The priests were to pronounce this blessing over the people of Israel and the synagogue; Christian liturgy continues to use it.

The blessing's three lines (vv. 24-27) build on an intricate poetic design involving a number of wordplays impossible to translate. Each line has one more word in it than the previous one, the first having three words and the last with five. The first line presents the simplest form: verb–YHWH–verb. Each line has a verb in the first position and YHWH in the second, while a verb also concludes the first and second lines. In the second and third lines the same words, "his-face upon-you," occur in the third place. Thus the concluding word, "peace," is the only word that breaks the precise pattern and hence is emphasized. This literal English translation indicates the Hebrew structure:

1	2	3	4	5
may-bless-you				
	YHWH			
		and-may-he-keep-you		
may-make-to-shine				
	YHWH			
		his-face upon-you		
			and-may-he-be-gracious-to-you	
may-lift-up				
	YHWH			
		his-face upon-you		
			and-may-he-give-you	
				peace.

54

How are we to understand the idea of a "blessing"? The custom of blessings has fallen out of favor today. We bless our food but probably little else. Any book of prayers has long lists of blessings. Parents blessed children, and there were regular blessings for planting, harvest, pregnant women, travelers, all kinds of events. Blessing is a concept central to the structure of the Pentateuch. After God creates man and woman, "God blessed them, and God said to them, 'Be fruitful and multiply, and fill the earth and subdue it; and have dominion over the fish of the sea and over the birds of the air and over every living thing that moves upon the earth' " (Gen. 1:28). What God says constitutes God's blessing. It concerns all the things of life. Deuteronomy 28:3-14 sets out a long list of God's blessings, "if you obey the LORD your God" (Deut. 28:2).

Curse is the opposite of blessing and once again Genesis provides the archetype of God's curse when God tells the man, "cursed is the ground because of you; in toil you shall eat of it all the days of your life. . . . By the sweat of your face you shall eat bread until you return to the ground, for out of it you were taken; you are dust, and to dust you shall return" (Gen. 3:17, 19). This curse exposes the essential difference between blessing and curse. Blessing represents life and curse represents death. As Moses tells the people in the covenant renewal liturgy, "I call heaven and earth to witness against you today that I have set before you life and death, blessings and curses. Choose life so that you and your descendants may live" (Deut. 30:19).

The second and third blessings (Num. 6:25-26) mention the "face" of God, an instance of the common Hebrew practice of an anthropomorphism. Most English translations obscure this repetition because in English such a device seems boring, although it is typical of Hebrew poetry, in which parallel patterns and sound establish rhythm. The face reflects the heart (Sir. 13:25; cf. Prov. 27:19). The mirror is a common metaphor for the face. Like the mirror, the face is both what is seen and what does the seeing. Being face-to-face was important in the ancient world because only by looking the other person in the eye could one judge the other person. For example, Plato distrusts written work because one cannot judge whether the author whom you cannot see, is telling the truth. The face is, then, a metaphor for the essence or soul of a person and hence can stand for the presence of a person. Thus to see God face-to-face (Ps. 51:11) or to see the face of God (Ps. 42:2) is to be in God's presence.

The stories of Moses' encounter with God illustrate these uses of "face" dramatically. Exodus 33 has two stories of Moses seeing the "face" of God. The first (Exod. 33:7-11) deals with Moses interceding for the people in the tent of meeting. When Moses would approach the tent, the people would stand outside and watch. "When all the people saw the pillar of cloud standing at the entrance of the tent, all the people would rise and bow down" (10). By way of contrast, "the LORD used to speak to Moses face to face, as one speaks to a friend" (11). Here Moses and Yahweh are presented as being on the most intimate terms. Intimacy with God requires Moses to veil his own face from the people, for his face reflects something the people cannot see. "Whenever Moses went in before the LORD to speak with him, he would take the veil off, until he came out" (Exod. 34:34).

In the next story in Exodus 33, Moses asks to see the "glory" of God, God's deepest essence. God responds, "you cannot see my face; for no one shall see me and live" (33:20). "Glory" and "face" are interchangeable terms here. God makes a counterproposal: "While my glory passes by I will put you in a cleft of the rock, and I will cover you with my hand until I have passed by; then I will take away my hand, and you shall see my back; but my face shall not be seen" (33:22-23). The slightly off-color humor of the passage effectively catches the Hebrew spirit and God's mocking response to Moses. This way of arguing is typical of the Bible. Biblical authors like to juxtapose two stories that are apparently contradictory and let the reader figure out how to navigate between them. Moses did speak to God as a friend, something no one else could do; but all he saw was God's rear.

The blessing employs the two different senses of "face." In the first, "make his face shine upon you" (Num. 6:25), the underlying image is the sun. Just as the sun gives life, so God's face shining on the people guarantees that they will have the fullness of life, hence life will be gracious, free, and easy. The second image connects "face" with sight. If Yahweh lifts up his face, he will see his people and, like a mighty warrior, will protect them, which leads to the conclusion, "he will give you peace."

The basic sense of Hebrew *shalom* (peace) is wholeness or well-being. It applies to material as well as spiritual and moral realities. Peace is always a gift of God (Ps. 29:11). Most significantly, peace and righteousness go together (Ps. 85:10; Isa. 32:17). Righteousness defines the relation between God and humanity. The righteous person is the one who is in the right relation with God and who therefore has peace. Such a person is indeed blessed.

Thus the blessing serves as a summary of the covenant and Hebrew religion. As important as the predicates are in this blessing, its center is the divine name Yahweh and the identification of God's name with the people. The people who bear the divine name are truly blessed.

SECOND LESSON: ROMANS 1:1-7; GALATIANS 4:4-7

The Second Sunday of Advent presented a reading from the opening of Philippians. In that context I discussed the characteristics of the opening of a Pauline letter. The Letter to the Romans corresponds to that form, except that the addresser section is considerably elaborated. Such elaboration is appropriate in this letter, because this is the only Pauline letter to a community that he did not found—he had to establish his credentials and identity with them.

The elaboration of the addresser is done in one periodic sentence that builds by placing in apposition a series of themes that link Paul to the Romans. The addresser is Paul alone, which is unusual in that Paul normally includes some of his co-workers. He uses three expressions to describe himself: "a slave [my translation] of Jesus," "called [by God implied] to be an apostle," and "set apart for the gospel of God." Each phrase conjures up an important and specific image. In the context of the Roman Empire, the term I translate as "slave" (usually translated "servant") invokes the lowest social class, to which many Christians probably belonged. While Roman slavery does not compare exactly with American slavery, it was the empire's soft underbelly. The Letter to Philemon testifies to the master's absolute power and the slave's desire to escape from it. "Apostle" stands in contrast to "slave" and indicates Paul's authority and his claim to status and recognition within the community. "Set apart" has a prophetic echo. In Paul's description of his calling in Galatians, he says that he was set apart from his mother's womb, echoing Isa. 49:1.

The "gospel of God" is described as promised beforehand by the Scriptures. Since a major element in the Roman Christian community is Jewish, this reference to the authority of the Jewish Scriptures is important, especially given Paul's reputation as one who has set aside the Torah, an argument that will take up considerable space in the letter. The gospel is about God's Son (v. 2); Paul then elaborates about the Son by employing a fragment of a Christian hymn. We have already discussed other hymnic fragments. This one is very primitive, employing terms in ways not at all common in other Pauline letters. Some have speculated that the hymn comes from the Roman community and is Paul's way of establishing a common bond in the faith with the community.

The hymn has a two-stage, sequential Christology built around the catchwords "in the flesh" and "in the spirit." In the flesh Jesus was the son of David, but by the resurrection he was exalted or appointed Son of God. Although the hymn in Hebrews has a similar pattern, this Roman fragment mentions no preexistence, unlike the Johannine prologue or the Philippians hymn, which probably represent a slightly later stage of development. Even later, toward the end of the first century, the letters of Ignatius combine these two traditions with the virgin birth to set up the pattern that will eventually lead to the patristic doctrine of the two natures of Christ. "There is one Physician, who is both flesh and spirit, born and yet not born, who is God in man, true life in death, both of Mary and of God" (*Ignatius to the Ephesians* 7:2).

The description of the gospel leads to the confession of Jesus as "Christ our Lord" (Rom. 1:4) and a shift in voice to "we" as a way of bonding with the letter's recipients (v. 5). Paul's apostleship, received from the Lord, has as its purpose to bring about the obedience of faith among the Gentiles, among whom are the Romans. This topic brings Paul full circle. He had begun by describing himself as a slave, that is, one subject to obedience. Now he describes the Romans as obedient to faith. He also had described himself as "called to be an apostle," and he ends by describing the Romans as "called to belong to Jesus Christ" (v. 6). Thus his description of himself parallels his description of them.

The lesson from Galatians comes from a section of the argument in which Paul is trying to demonstrate the freedom of the children of God over against what he considers to be their enslavement in submitting to circumcision. The immediate argument derives from the Christian experience of baptism (Gal. 3:26-29). "Baptized into union with him, you have all put on Christ like a garment" (3:27, REB). If the Christian belongs to Christ, "you are the 'issue' of Abraham and heirs by virtue of the promise" (3:29, REB). This verse concludes this section of the argument. Paul now advances a proof drawn from everyday life (4:1-2) and then applies it to the Christian story (4:3-7).

Even though verses 1-3 fall outside today's reading, the reading makes little sense without these verses. Paul's argument relies on the status of heirs in the Hellenistic world. Because of the *Potestas Patri* (the power of the father), the members of the father's household were held in virtual slavery. Even the heir was no better than a slave until the heir received the inheritance. Then he in his right would have the *Potestas Patri*. This state, Paul concludes, is that of everyone before the coming of Christ and baptism. Though heirs, they are enslaved to "the elemental spirits of the universe" (4:3), which are those demonic powers that control the world. In Hellenism these powers were the astral deities or Fate (*Tychē*). This statement, applied to the individual, does represent Paul's thinking. Apart from faith, every person, whether Gentile or Jew, stands under the judgment of the elemental spirits. But applying this judgment temporally can cause a distortion of Paul's thought, a distortion that he was at pains to point out in Romans 4. Since Abraham is saved by faith, the gospel and faith are not isolated to Christianity but events of grace always present in the world.

The opposite of enslavement to the elemental spirits is faith in Christ. In Gal. 4:4 "the fullness of time" (NRSV, NAB) or "the appointed time" (REB) is an apocalyptic expression denoting the conclusion of history. Again, one should not view it as representing a temporal sequence but as indicating the redemption of history itself. That Jesus is God's son is critical for Paul's argument because only a son could inherit. By analogy, the Christian is adopted as a son. In its effort to present an inclusive translation, the NRSV translates the critical phrase as "children" and thus obscures the parallel with Jesus. Jesus was born of a woman, under the law, just like us. As a son of God he is the heir, but redemption/adoption makes us sons of God and therefore heirs with Christ. Precisely because we are like Christ, we can cry out at baptism, our new birth, "Abba"—God is our daddy. This cry of liberation belongs to all Christians. We are no longer bound to the elemental spirits of any kind—we are free. We are the heirs to the world, not its slaves or prisoners.

GOSPEL: LUKE 2:15-21

Today's Gospel reading completes the birth story in Luke's Gospel. It has two parts: first the signs of the birth's manifestation (2:15-20), then Jesus' naming (2:21).

The shepherds' responding to the message of the angel provides a frame around a scene of Jesus' birth in poverty. The shepherds as representatives of the poor, the marginalized, are the first recipients and proclaimers of the gospel, for they receive, investigate, and proclaim the message to others, who are amazed at what the shepherds have to say. Mary treasures these things in her heart, that is, she thinks about them, for they will make sense to her only after the resurrection.

The circumcision and naming of the child were important religious and cultural ceremonies. Luke makes nothing of either event, except to note that they happened. The circumcising of the male child marks off that child as a member of the covenantal community; it was and still is a time of great celebration for the family and a sign of pride in being Jewish. Along with Sabbath observance, it has continued to be a distinctive sign of the Jew. During the early Hellenistic period Antiochus Epiphanes (175–164 B.C.E.) made circumcision a capital offense which led to a number of martyrdoms (1 Macc. 1:20-63). Again the forbidding of circumcision under the Roman emperor Hadrian was a major element in provoking the Bar Kokhba revolt (132–135 C.E.).

Luke likewise makes nothing of the name of Jesus. By contrast, Matthew plays on the popular derivation of Jesus' Hebrew name. The angel announces that the child is to be named Jesus and then provides an explanation of the name: "he will save his people from their sins" (Matt. 1:21). This interpretation is based on a Hebrew wordplay. The Greek name *Iēsous* derives ultimately from the Hebrew *yĕhôshûa'* (Joshua), but more immediately from the contracted form *yēshûa'*. This contracted form sounds like the Hebrew word for salvation or help (*yĕshûâ*) which in turn gave rise to the popular derivation of Jesus: "Yahweh saves."

The social significance of the naming of the child is that Joseph accepts the child as his own. It is the celebration of the child's legitimization.

Second Sunday after Christmas

Lutheran	Roman Catholic	Episcopal	Revised Common
Isa. 61:10—62:3	Sir. 24:1-2, 8-12	Jer. 31:7-14	Jer. 31:7-14 or Sir. 24:1-12
Eph. 1:3-6, 15-18	Eph. 1:3-6, 15-18	Eph. 1:3-6, 15-19a	Eph. 1:3-14
John 1:1-18	John 1:1-18 or John 1:1-5, 9-14	Matt. 2:13-15, 19-23 or Luke 2:41-52	John 1:(1-9),10-18

FIRST LESSON

Isaiah 61:10—62:3

Isaiah 61 is an exilic poem of a type that we saw frequently during Advent. Its first verse announces its theme: "The spirit of the Lord GOD is upon me, because the LORD has anointed me; he has sent me to bring good news to the oppressed." The first reading today is taken from the poem's conclusion in which the prophet-singer thanks God in advance for the deliverance of the people. The exuberance of the singer breaks out in a welter of metaphors. He is first like a bridegroom, then a bride, and finally a blooming garden. The underlying fertility metaphors are obvious and recall the Garden of Eden. Salvation gives the people new life. The androgynous metaphors indicate a breakdown of one of the strongest boundaries of the ancient world.

Isaiah 62 is also a complete poem that celebrates the liberation of Jerusalem. Unfortunately the reading truncates the poem just as it is about to give the bride Jerusalem's new name, in which the bridegroom takes delight: "But you shall be called 'My Delight,' and your land 'Espoused' " (Isa. 62:4, NAB).

Jeremiah 31:7-14

The reading from Jeremiah comes from the first part of a section termed the Book of Consolation (30:1—31:40), part of which formed the first lesson for the First Sunday of Advent and an alternative reading on the First Sunday after Christmas. It celebrates the Lord's ransoming and redeeming Jacob "from hands too strong for him" (Jer. 31:11). It too concludes with a joyful image of the young dancing and the old making merry (v. 13). These images of joyful celebration of the Lord's faithfulness to the covenant cannot just be transferred willy-nilly to the Christian community. We are not the "remnant of Israel" mentioned in verse 7. In this season when we celebrate the Savior's coming, we must always remind ourselves that if the promises made to Israel remain unfulfilled, God is unfaithful and Jesus is not the Messiah. A supersessionist theology that replaces Israel with the church may be easier to digest, but it displaces a faithful God for a fickle God.

Sirach 24:1-12

Sirach is one of those books with the ambiguous status of being canonical for some in the Christian tradition and noncanonical for others. The book is frequently referred to either as Sirach or Ecclesiasticus (not Ecclesiastes, a Hebrew wisdom book that is part of the canon). Sirach is the standard Greek title for the book and Ecclesiasticus is the Vulgate (Jerome's Latin translation) title, which means "the church book." Most Greek manuscripts bear the title "The Wisdom of Jesus the Son of Sirach." The book was originally written in Hebrew in Jerusalem around 180 B.C.E., but never made it into the Hebrew canon; hence the Reformers rejected it. The book was revered in Jewish circles until the medieval period. It has survived in Hebrew fragments both from the storeroom of the Cairo synagogue and in the Dead Sea Scrolls.

The text that is translated today as part of the Apocrypha or deuterocanonical books belongs to the LXX canon and thus the canon of the Catholic church. It was translated into Greek around 132 B.C.E. by Jesus' grandson, who lived in Egypt. The grandson even added a foreword celebrating his grandfather: "A legacy of great value has come down to us through the law, the prophets, and the writers who followed in their steps, and Israel deserves recognition for its traditions of learning and wisdom. . . . My grandfather Jesus . . . was moved to compile a book of his own on the themes of learning and wisdom, in order that, with this further help, scholars might make greater progress in their studies by living as the law directs" (REB). The grandson also includes some words of warning for those who would interpret the Scriptures without being able to read the original languages. "For what is said in Hebrew does not have the same force when translated into another tongue. Not only the present work, but even the law itself, as well as the prophets and the other writings, are not a little different when spoken in the original" (REB).

The Hymn of Wisdom (24:1-22) parallels that of Prov. 8:22—9:12, and in general the wisdom of Jesus ben Sirach falls well within the Israelite wisdom tradition. Wisdom is "the word spoken by the Most High" (Sir. 24:3, REB), a phrase that the hymnic prologue of the Fourth Gospel echoes. Wisdom is responsible for creation, and eventually the creator God commands Wisdom, whom he created, "Make your home in Jacob" (v. 8). Wisdom dwells among Jacob: "In the sacred tent I ministered in his presence," again a phrase echoed by John's prologue. But this dwelling differs from that of the Word in the Fourth Gospel. There the Word becomes a human being, not just the sacred presence among the people. This is a move well beyond any made in the wisdom tradition.

SECOND LESSON: EPHESIANS 1:3-6, 15-18

Today's second lesson is something of a pastiche in the various lectionaries, except in the Revised Common Lectionary. One hopes, I suspect in vain, that the pastiche does not do too much damage.

Although the authorship of Ephesians is debated, the tendency today is to see the letter as pseudonymous, written not by Paul but by a pupil of Paul sometime shortly after his death (see, for example, Ralph P. Martin, *Ephesians, Colossians, and Philemon*, Interpretation [Louisville: Westminster/John Knox, 1991]). The letter was written to communities that Paul did not found; it was probably a circular letter intended for a number of communities in Asia Minor. It makes virtually no references to specific circumstances or controversies, as the genuine Pauline letters do.

The letter begins with praise of God, who has predestined believers to be the adopted children of God. The function of this predestination is that it should "redound to his praise" (1:6, REB).

In the second part of the lesson, the author gives thanks and prays that all may have "the spiritual gifts of wisdom and vision" (REB; NRSV, "revelation") in order to know God and that "the inward eyes may be enlightened" (REB) to know the hope offered. This hope is the inheritance of the adopted children for which they were predestined. The proof of this inheritance is Christ's resurrection from the dead (v. 20), which indicates that the inheritance is creation itself, over which Christ has been given sovereignty.

GOSPEL: JOHN 1:1-18; LUKE 2:41-52

This was the lesson for Christmas Day, hence the reader can consult that section for the appropriate remarks. Those who use the Episcopal lectionary selection of Luke 2:41-52 should refer to the First Sunday after Christmas.

Today's three lessons recapitulate themes that have been enunciated throughout Advent, Christmas, and the following Sundays: the faithfulness of God to his covenant with Israel; salvation involves the whole of creation and the place of Christianity in society. Each generation of Christians has to work out anew Yahweh's claim on creation and what faithfulness to the covenant means. Some ways these questions have been worked out in the tradition are wrong, even if mindlessly repeated today (for example, supersessionism, or "the world is evil"). In the new global village, we must face again God's covenant with creation and its implications. As far as I can tell, the Bible offers no answer, only a series of stories that try to work out these themes. Like a musical score, the Bible is often variations on a theme, rather than one note. A preacher could not wish for a greater set of themes on which to preach over a cycle. But be assured that the theme is more important and enduring than the answer.

metaphor: figure of speech in which a term is transferred from the object it ordinarily designates to an object it may designate only by implicit comparison or analogy (the evening of life) / figurative language, allegory, parable

implicit: implied or understood although not directly expressed / inherent or contained in the nature of something although not directly expressed / having no doubts or reservations, understood unquestioning